MW00990340

Cover Design: Gregory Martin and Ashley Berges

Library of Congress Cataloging-in-Publication Data
Berges, Ashley, 1978-
Live Your True Life : A guide to a successful life journey
Ashley Berges
ISBN 978-0-615-38432-0 (alk. paper)

Originally Published in Texas by LYTL Inc., 2010
ISBN 978-0-615-38432-0

LT
Publishing

I want to dedicate this book to my husband Greg Fasullo for all his patience and understanding. He is conscious of my determination to help others understand themselves and their chosen journey. I want to thank my mom, Juneria Berges. She has always been there for me. She has read and listened to my theories, philosophies, my thoughts on the world, mankind, and my life philosophy since I was five. Every paper I wrote depicting my new theories on value definitions, consciousness, etc., she always read with a smile and always had questions and thoughts to really show she cared no matter how tedious the subject. I want to thank my dad, John Berges. He has always made me smile and taught me to lighten-up now and then. I want to thank Gregory Martin for keeping me on a time line and for Pure Magazine for showing me just how many people are looking for knowledge and understanding on this subject. And for my grandmother, Syble, she has unimaginable depth and will but through it all has the sweet and innocent laughter of a schoolgirl.

LIVE YOUR TRUE LIFE

A GUIDE TO A SUCCESSFUL
LIFE JOURNEY

Ashley Berges

2-1-2011

Dear Terri -
Keep up the good work!
You are a wonderful example
for others!
Can't wait to work with you.
Love, Ashley :)

INTRODUCTION:
LIVE YOUR TRUE LIFE

When I wrote "Live Your True Life", I left one part for last - the introduction. I knew it needed to grab your attention as well as introduce and define this book. I went to great lengths and spent long hours slumped over my laptop while attempting to knock out the 'perfect' introduction. It didn't seem a simple task, because honestly, I was complicating it quite a bit more than necessary. But as I diligently worked through my thoughts, I realized the book was in fact easily introduced! It's funny how something so simple can seem insurmountable, but only in my mind. As soon as I stepped back to view my situation, of course I could easily see the next step ahead.

"Live Your True Life" is, indeed, defined by its title - living true to oneself is clearly the conceptual meat of these chapters. It's about being able to clearly observe, carefully contemplate, and continuously correct what isn't proving productive with unflinching honesty. Every single one of us has at least one troubling weakness that's difficult to overcome, right? This book is dedicated to each person who wants to overcome that obstacle. Let's work together to resolve the issues that have been so neglected in the busyness of our day-to-day lives. Think of this book as a straightforward guide and quick read to refer to often. "Live Your True Life" will help you and remind you to reflect on and address your problem issues, often by giving a fresh perspective, and by placing you on a path to personal clarity.

This book is not long, or tedious to read, and it doesn't require a knowledge of world history starting from the beginning of time. It simply sheds light on who we are and what makes us truly happy. It was written with you, the reader, in mind - the reader with the busy schedule who doesn't need another time-consuming chore. It's a simple and sincerely written read meant to help sort through life's events, how to deal with these situations, and how to resolve them and grow in the process.

Think of "Live Your True Life" as a manual that provides directions for pursuing and finding happiness in all facets of life while maximizing the value of our precious time on this earth. Think of it as a guide for acquiring and maintaining a happy and healthy life. Think of it as a guide to personal enlightenment, empowerment, and clarity. It offers a blueprint for achieving balance, success, happiness, and inner peace in all aspects of life. The trick to overcoming obstacles is recognizing that no matter how difficult they seem, they can be changed, moved, reversed, and even completely wiped out. Maintaining a policy of truth to self and truth to others creates an environment for the life we were created to live. Living true facilitates productivity and prosperity, and what follows is a more peaceful world.

Even on a subconscious level, we inherently know what's best for us when we allow ourselves to think clearly and feel fully. We each learn about life in a deeply personal way, and certain lessons can only be learned "the hard way". Many fall into patterns such as making the same mistakes over and over, approaching the same situation in the same manner, thinking about it the same way, behaving the same way, and then expecting a different outcome! Obviously life doesn't successfully flourish this way, invariably it leads to disappointment and frustration.

Recognizing the need for fundamental change is

the first step to living the life we deserve and desire. This change extends to attitudes, thoughts, and ultimately behavior patterns. I wrote "Live Your True Life" to create a positive impact on the world in which we live - by transforming lives. Even the smallest change can bring about a substantial impact, starting with our own lives and then affecting the lives of others around us. In theory we all possess this skill, this ability to recognize the changes required in thoughts and behaviors - but we must achieve personal clarity to identify our issues before we can expect to change.

Some of the information in the book may be familiar to you, some might be new, and some will reinforce concepts that you may previously have been acquainted with. We all know much about ourselves and the world we inhabit subconsciously and intuitively; hopefully this book will bring much of that to consciousness.

Personal growth is something that must happen daily. Like anything else, not moving forward is stagnating or reversing and that isn't a powerful or positive situation in our lives. Continual stimulation and renewal even in everyday circumstances will make our lives fruitful and complete. We'll be able to grow and pursue the happiness we desire instead of always longing for something we think we want.

Personal enlightenment is critical to clearly see why we do what we do and what we think we're trying to gain. But it can be most challenging because it requires that we look within ourselves and evaluate how we think and feel. When we search within we're able to see those same mistakes we make, and why we may play the same losing card time after time.

This is transformational - achieving personal enlightenment can lead to a path of lasting satisfaction. Personal enlightenment requires us to slow down and honestly contemplate our actions. When we understand why we do what we do and be able to look at our life options with complete clarity and understanding, then we can calmly observe ourselves without making judgments and understand who we truly are. Personal enlightenment allows us to be ourselves on solid ground, and eliminate self-sabotaging routines and behaviors.

Personal clarity is also key - it puts the true picture of personal growth and enlightenment into focus. Living a life that remains true to oneself and others is the lens through which events can be seen for what they truly are. Clarity is also the ability to see oneself as objectively as possible - our strengths and weaknesses without a mask or cover-up.

When you pick up "Live Your True Life", remember that you don't have to read the entire book tonight. In fact, I suggest you don't. Read a few chapters and put it down. The next time you come back to it, perhaps go back over the chapters you read, then consider sharing your thoughts with others, journaling or blogging on the subjects you read about and only then move on to the next chapter. I kept this book short in length so it's not too overwhelming, time-consuming or another potential obstacle in your day. The basic concepts we'll explore are timeless – just as current and relevant today as they were 2000 years ago. So take as much or as little time as you need to read and absorb the information, go at your own pace, and enjoy the time you're dedicating to the improvement and cultivation of your magnificent original life.

The most important thing to remember is to put the concepts discussed into practice and use them everyday. You'll quickly find life easier, happier, healthier, and much more fun! My hope is that "Live

LIVE YOUR TRUE LIFE

Your True Life" will help you find ways of navigating your life through personal growth, enlightenment, and clarity. Life doesn't have to be difficult, it can be a dynamic and exciting journey that you may just be beginning or perhaps continuing. Either way, this book will help you proceed in a positive direction.

Of course at the end of the day, a book is just a book. An inanimate object of recorded thoughts and feelings in the form of words typed on paper in a binding. These words can't just jump up off the pages by themselves. To change lives, they must be put into action. Along with practicing the "Live Your True Life" concepts, I highly recommend lively discussions with others. This illuminates our ideas and conclusions, thereby teaching others through our insights as well as learning from their experiences.

All in all, we are a conscious collective that can work together to create a wonderfully positive and advanced civilization, living by our ideals and continuing to spiritually advance, because we are constantly striving to better ourselves instead of competing against one another. "Live Your True Life" is not just a book, it is also the basis for the "Live Your True Life" online community, www.liveyourtruelife.org, where you can create your own personal profile and meet other readers to share your ideas and thoughts.

If you would like to share your life-changing story, give feedback, or share how "Live Your True Life" has benefited you, I would love to hear from you at liveyourtruelife@me.com.

Again, I hope you will keep this book and refer to it often for years to come and I hope it helps to bring you a more peaceful and happy life.

Table of Contents

Introduction: 11

Chapter 1:   Your Time and Energy are Important   23

Chapter 2:   Dealing With Negative,   37
               Energy-Suckers in your life

Chapter 3:   What are You Doing Right Now?   49
               The Mindful Mind vs. The Thinking Mind

Chapter 4:   Expectations Are Overrated   57

Chapter 5:   Do you Love Yourself?   65

Chapter 6:   Be Yourself and by the Way,   83
               Who Are You?

Chapter 7:   Time Travel, Do you have   97
               a Time Machine

Table of Contents

Chapter 8:   You Are What You Eat,   113
              You Are What You See and Hear

Chapter 9:   Doing What is Right for You...   137
              Within Moderation

Final Word: 155

LIVE YOUR TRUE LIFE

Chapter 1:

YOUR TIME AND ENERGY ARE IMPORTANT!

The three main reasons we must place boundaries are to protect our time, our energy, and our physical and or emotional space. Time doesn't stop and because of that, we have to prioritize what we want to spend our time doing. Most of the time, we use our time on work, family, spouse, children, friends, and we forget ourselves in the process. In order for you to be a happy and healthy person, you must take time for yourself. That might mean spending one hour reading a book, watching your favorite television program, taking a walk, working out, meditating, or any another activity that you especially like, that comforts you, revitalizes you, and centers you.

Just as important as your time is your energy. You can't achieve your goals in life if you have no energy to give to them. When we use our energy on things that aren't on our priority list, we have less energy to do the things that are important to us. When we set good boundaries, we spend our time and energy wisely and with personal intent. By placing and following through with good boundaries, we don't waste time and energy with people, activities, food, etc that aren't good for us. Our personal and emotional space is very important and in order to maintain that space, we must place boundaries when someone is acting or behaving in a way that is not beneficial to us. Having personal and emotional space is healthy in all relationships. A relationship with no boundaries has the tendency to run its course and dissolve quicker than a healthy relationship that was set up with boundaries and the understanding of each other's personal and emotional space.

We have trouble standing up for ourselves sometimes. We've all agreed to do things we don't want to do, and we've all tolerated things we didn't want to tolerate. For the most part, we do these things because we don't want to deal with conflict and we want everyone to like us. Unfortunately, without proper boundaries in a relationship, conflict will generally ensue at some point. This conflict can result in a situation that can be more difficult to overcome than would have, with the establishment of proper boundaries originally. When we start a new relationship with boundaries, we allow it to grow in a healthy and mature manner that provides equally for all involved.

A boundary, in this context, is the emotional and or physical space between you and another person. In order to stop the cycle of unhappy and unhealthy living, we must learn how to set boundaries. Because the purpose of a boundary is to protect and take care of ourselves, we must be able to set boundaries and further more, stick to our boundaries. We have the right to protect and defend ourselves when someone is acting in a way or doing something that is not acceptable. We have to take personal responsibility for how others treat us. When others are not treating us appropriately, we have the right and obligation to speak up, in hopes of changing the situation.

In the beginning of any relationship, it is best to start with simple but firm boundaries that you can express in your normal tone of voice.

An example of a simple boundary: You don't allow people to drop by your house uninvited. If this were a boundary of yours, you would need to make your friends aware that they need to always call before dropping by your house.

Another example, you don't accept phone calls after 11pm on the weekdays, unless it is an emergency, due to your early work schedule. You will need to make your friends and family aware, so they can respect your boundaries.

Other types of boundaries are not as simple and might involve emotional space instead of just the physical space.

Part 1: Accurate description of actions and behaviors by that person and how it makes you feel. When dealing with more complex boundaries, we must use more description to allow the other person to understand and see the situation through our eyes. Many times, we must set boundaries due to other's actions and behaviors. The boundaries that we must set in order to stop these behaviors and actions must be as descriptive as possible in order to communicate our wishes and needs. An example of a more complex and accurately described boundary is: When you look at me with that frown on your face and your brows are furrowed and you turn away and laugh, it makes me feel sad. I feel that you are disappointed with me and laughing at me, I want you to stop. These facial expressions are a symptom or evidence of an underlying problem that this particular person has with you. You can't control what happens on other's faces but you can find out the reason for it and either accept it or not allow this attitude/behavior around you. When you are talking with that person, you must describe to them the actions that are making you feel uncomfortable.

Part 2: Find the reason for this attitude and or actions and a solution

You begin by stating the problem. That normally begins with a 'when you' statement that is followed by the actions of that person. Remember that you are not the emotion, so instead of saying I am hurt; you state, "I feel hurt because of your actions". And hopefully, this begins an honest discussion about the underlying problem and begins correction of the attitude and actions of this person.

Part 3:   Boundary Enforcement

Just as important as setting boundaries is the enforcement of your boundaries. The third part is for you. You don't need to tell the other person what it is that you will do if they don't abide by your boundary but you will know the action or actions you will take, if they don't.

Why do we need boundaries?

Boundaries help us prioritize where we spend our time and energy; therefore, when we begin forming boundaries, we must think about our priorities.

Life Priorities:
- Spouse/Family
- Friends
- Pets
- Home
- Health
- Job/Money
- Charity
- Fun/Relaxation

This list is different for everyone but in order to prioritize our time and energy, we need to know our priorities.

Boundaries keep us on track with our lives and protect our time and energy so we can pursue our true-life goals.

Where to use boundaries:

- Friendships
- Marriage
- Work
- Associates
- Family

Most of us don't have many, if any, boundaries in place. We choose this for many reasons and thankfully we can change it. With practice, we can positively place practical boundaries to help us use our energy and time for our true goals and desires. We all have a choice with everything we do, or don't do. Since we own our choices, we are already empowered to begin taking responsibility for our lives.

All of us have wished for more time in a day. I used to say that daily, wondering where the day went.
I love interacting with people and love talking with others as well, but I realized that I was losing my time to get things done. It wasn't until these conversations would make me late to meetings or family functions that I realized I had to change something. I decided to change my mode of operation. So the next day, I went through the office lobby and as usual engaged in a conversation. Knowing that I had a meeting in twenty minutes, and that I still had to drive to it, I thought about my options.

Options:
1. Forget about how late I would be for the meeting and talk
2. Run through the lobby with my head down and a newspaper covering my face so they don't see me

3. Stop them before they can get a word out and tell them I'm in a hurry

4. Say hello and converse for five minutes, explain I have a meeting, if they continue to talk, remind them of my meeting, and if this conversation is truly important, ask them to call or email me about it, when they get the time.

Option 4 allows me to make my meeting and not be late. It also allows me to be polite, personable, and receive information. And if I truly needed to know the information or just wanted to know, we can converse when everyone has the time to listen. I realize that this is a rather simple issue and it had a simple solution but sometimes the right choice is not obvious, and needs more thought and follow through action.

I realize that some boundaries might seem easier to express than others but everything takes time to work towards and to get more comfortable with. When we deal with people we love, it can be difficult to set boundaries because we are scared that they might get angry or not love us anymore. We are all allowed to have boundaries and if someone truly loves you, they will understand, accept, and respect your boundaries.

Setting your own personal boundaries:

Throughout our lives, we all have done things for others and in the middle of doing these things, become resentful. We become resentful because we aren't working on our own overdue projects, and we aren't taking care of our own business. When we find ourselves in these situations, we tend to get angry but not change our ways. The next times you find yourself in a similar situation remember that this situation doesn't help anyone.

When you do something, you should want to do it and be a positive participant in the process. Sometimes however we don't always know what we are committing to with respect to the scope or scale of the commitment. In every situation, we must fully discuss the project with all involved prior to taking on the project. Unfortunately even the most thought out project can take a turn and we must allow for error. But with any commitment, we must choose wisely and with clear thought and purpose. When you have a million things to do, and you take on something else that you don't need to be doing, you will be going through the motions, possibly become overwhelmed or resentful and, overall, doing nobody, and especially yourself, any good. It is not another's fault that we become overwhelmed or resentful for taking on another project that we had no business taking on in the first place.

By placing boundaries and being able to say no, the things that you say yes to become that much more important. We should be extremely careful about when we say yes to something; once we say yes we should be committed, so we shouldn't be resentful about it. Remember you ultimately choose where you spend your time and energy. The next time someone asks you to take on another project you must carefully evaluate the work you already have in front of you. Before agreeing to action, its best to think about the project, the time it will take you, etc. and get back to that person the next day so you don't just agree without truly focusing on your responsibilities you already have. It's better to say no then to take on something that will make you feel resentment or stress and ultimately cause a rift between you and the other person.

Personal Reflection and Blog:

Questions to think about and truthfully answer for yourself and your growth.

1. Are there areas in your life where boundaries need to be established?

2. Are their friends or family that you need to sit down with and have a dialogue on particular actions and behaviors?

3. Do you sometimes feel that you have put yourself on the back burner because you are always doing things for other people?

4. Occasionally, do you agree to do things and not follow through because you have overcommitted?

5. Do you catch yourself racing around to make all your commitments even when you aren't feeling well?

6. Do you say yes too quickly to a request and then later wished you could take it back?

If you answered yes to any of the above questions, you need to work on establishing and keeping true to your boundaries. Creating positive boundaries will be an important factor in bettering your life. When we develop and implement positive boundaries in our lives, we allow our lives to be true and more fulfilling. We also allow ourselves the time and energy to put toward those goals we have for ourselves.

At this time, begin a journal or notebook.

On page one, write the word boundaries and underneath write down the boundaries you have created for yourself. If there are any that you want to establish write those below the currently executed boundaries.

Turn the page, in order to give you enough space for the new boundaries you wish to establish. On the next page write down the boundaries you have created between you and others. Define the boundary and list with who or whom you have created this boundary. Just like before, if there are boundaries that you wish to establish, write those down below the currently executed boundaries.

Keeping track of your efforts is a wonderfully positive exercise that is rewarding and beneficial. Journaling, in this way, allows us to take charge of our life and reaffirm our life direction.

Chapter 2:

DEALING WITH NEGATIVE, ENERGY. SUCKERS IN YOUR LIFE

Negativity is not fun! Negativity sucks the positive energy out of anything. It is very difficult to be positive when others around you are being negative. We've all been around people who are perpetually negative. These same people, due to their negativity, can rob us of our energy – they become energy suckers. Some of those same people are never happy and something bad is always happening to them. I have a friend that is always negative. One day he called, began talking, and he didn't stop talking for an hour. By the end of the conversation, I was feeling worn out and sad. I felt drained of all my energy and vowed to not take a call from him until I knew how to handle it. After that conversation, I realized that I had to set up a defense or help my friend reevaluate his situation to see clearly instead of through brown tinted glasses.

Bad stuff happens to everyone but we can choose to dwell on it or move past it. Unfortunately, for people that are negative, they don't re-focus, they continue to focus on the bad things and let the good things pass them by. In turn, by being around them, we can become tired, weak, or even sick.

If you do not have a strategy for dealing with these energy-suckers they will suck all of your energy and leave you feeling sick and run-down. Most of the time when people do this, you don't realize it has happened until it's too late. In order to protect yourself and your energy, you must be able to identify the energy-suckers in your life and know how to stop them from taking your energy. Because there is no sign hanging over their head that states energy-sucker in big red letters, we must learn to identify them by the way we feel when we are around them. You must begin by recognizing your feelings and physical symptoms when you are around these energy suckers.

How To Identify that you are with an Energy Sucker:

1. You feel tense or guarded around them
2. You can't wait to get away from them
3. You began your time with them feeling very energetic, but quickly lose your energy, and even begin to feel ill

4. You feel confined or constricted with them

5. You feel you are under attack or constant scrutiny with them

6. You feel some muscle tension and headache

If so, you are probably dealing with a negative person who is sucking your energy.

Once you are able to identify the energy-suckers in your life, you can begin working on strategies to maintain your energy level and positive attitude when you are in their presence.

HOW TO DEAL WITH NEGATIVE PEOPLE

First off, we must remember that people have to make changes for themselves; we can't make changes for them. You can explain, tell, and show by example, but you can't make someone that is negative become positive without that person wanting to make that change. With that understanding, some people in our lives are negative and possibly won't change. When dealing with them, remember how they are and remember to stay positive. Remember, if you aren't able to guard from that person's negativity, keep your time around them to a minimum. Negativity can be contagious, so remember to consciously wash your hands when you are around it and don't let it come home with you, it's always looking for another host.

12. Strategies for dealing with negative people:

1. Try to identify why they are being negative. If you can understand where it is coming from, it's always much easier to deal with it.

2. Don't allow their negativity to get under your skin. Don't give them emotion to feed. When negativity begins don't add to it. Don't react to their negativity in any way. Remember to be a conscious observer, sit back and observe. When we follow the way of the conscious observer, we don't act, instead we sit back and observe others in order to understand the situation we currently find ourselves in. Most importantly, by being the conscious observer, you know and understand that this negativity and unhappiness is not yours. You don't own it; so don't take ownership of it!

3. With one negative story must come one positive story. After you have sat in conscious observation and listened to one negative situation, ask the person to tell you something positive that has happened for them lately. This can do two different

things. It can make the other person realize just how negative they are being and possibly begin to make a change, or it can make them stop going to you to share their negative stories.

4. Ask them about their next step — do they have a solution to their problem? If it seems that they're inundating you with a grocery list of issues, ask them what they're going to do to change the situation. Dwelling on negative situations keeps us from truly changing to make our lives better it's always better to focus on the solutions rather than dwelling on the problems. This may require you to go step by step through the situation in order to help someone arrive at a solution When we are just focusing on a negative situation, we aren't truly focusing on changing that situation and making our life better, we are just focusing on the problem.

5. Have a heart to heart with them about how you feel. In life, we want to give people the benefit of the doubt. Maybe they are not aware of how negative they are being. Perhaps they don't realize that their behavior and attitude is affecting you. Calmly talk to them and explain the behavior and attitudes that are affecting you adversely. Allow them to respond and listen to what they have to

say. Are they accepting ownership for their attitude and behavior or do they defend their behavior by attacking and placing blame on you?

6. Employ your Affirmations to keep yourself on positive target. Affirmations are positive statements that we create and use to enforce a desired outcome. When faced with adversity and negativity, many times we get off target and fall into the trap of negativity and hopelessness. In order to stay focused and on a positive target, we must develop and employ working affirmations. In order to develop proper and working affirmations, they must be in the present tense, express a positive statement, and be short and to the point. Example: I am creating a positive space for others and myself.

7. Visualize and deploy your protective shield. Your protective shield against negativity is what you visualize it to be. In order to create a working and powerful shield, the use of visualizations is important. In the recent movie, "The Incredibles", Violet is able to generate a special force field around her and others for the use of protection. The classic DC Comics heroine, Wonder Woman used her protective bracelets to deflect attacks. In Star Wars, deflector shields are standard issue on most all ships

in the universe. These deflector shields guarded against all types of attacks. These examples of protective shields allow us to visualize our own shield for dealing with negativity and emotional attack. When surrounded with negativity, visualize your protective shield and remember to deploy and keep activated when needed. Remember that you are a positive good person that has a protection shield around you. You are protected from the negative flow because it can't penetrate the shield you have created for yourself. When people make negative, nasty comments to you, visualize them hitting that protective shield and being thrown off.

8. People can be our mirrors. When we listen to others talk about their own emotional issues, we can get angry, it might push our buttons, and we might allow it to get under our skin. Why are we allowing those things to get to us? Sometimes the people that push our buttons the most can be good teachers. These people can serve as a mirror and help us to learn about ourselves. When we see things in others that we don't like, it should compel us to search within ourselves for those similar traits. We tend to see other's problems or issues before we see our own. Either way, the other person's traits are adversely affecting you and because of that, you

must go within yourself and see why you are affected. Mirrors can be our family, friends, coworkers, etc. The mirrors in our lives can change and repeat. Mirrors are there for us to learn about ourselves, so if we aren't learning about ourselves, we will continue to receive repeating mirrors. These mirrors keep giving us the same image to learn from. Once we begin to identify the mirrors in our life and we learn from them, our relationships with others will grow stronger and we will grow as a person.

9. The weight of the world is not on your shoulders. You are not everyone's psychologist; you don't have to solve everyone's problems. You can listen consciously, but you don't have to fix everything for everyone. People have to figure out and possibly fix things on their own; you can help but you can't do it for them.

10. Listen to your breathing and take deep breaths. When we are completely engaged in a situation, we have a tendency to forget to take good healthy breaths. When you remember to take healthy deep breaths, you are making a conscious effort to concentrate on your breathing. When you concentrate on your breathing, you are able to take inventory of how your body is feeling in any

given situation. When you are listening, remember that you can listen and breathe at the same time. Remember that with every internal breath, breathe in the positive and with every external breath, expel the negative. When around negative people, there is a tendency to feel tired or even sick, but when you are paying attention to your breathing, you won't be giving all of your energy away and you will be able to stay more centered. Please reference chapter three for strategies to maintaining your positive energy level.

11. Get up and move around. When you are in these situations, excusing yourself for a few minutes and moving around helps you to reenergize, and see the situation at hand more clearly. You need to recharge and refresh at least once an hour. Putting distance between you and the situation allows you to see things more clearly. This allows you to come back refueled, refreshed, and renewed.

12. If all else fails, pull the cord. Sometimes certain people are no longer beneficial to our lives and can keep us from achieving our goals. These people need endless financial, emotional, and mental support but are insensitive to you and your needs. When you are constantly giving and not receiving, you must

ask yourself why you feel the obligation to stay in this relationship. Even long-standing relationships can run their course and may be hindering you from achieving your goals and desires. Feeling obligated to an unhealthy relationship is counterproductive to you and your life.

Personal Reflection and Blog:

With regards to the 12 strategies, how have you put them into daily practice?

Who are the mirrors in your life?
What part of you are they mirroring?
At what point did you realize this person is a mirror to you?
What work have you done to positively change your life with respect to this habit or trait that was being mirrored?

In your journal/notebook, turn to a new page and list the people that you contract the energy sucker symptoms from when you are around them.
The next time you are with these people, use the techniques and see how they work with each person. List the name of each person and underneath the

name list the techniques that worked.

If there are any people on the list that none of the techniques worked, ask yourself why do you spend time with this person? Sometimes the most difficult people to move from are those we have known the longest. You must really examine these relationships and decide if at any time have these relationships been beneficial. Are they still beneficial? If not, then what is their role in your life? Are they a mirror? What are they mirroring? If they are not, you need to begin the process of moving on. Unfortunately, for the most part, having these elements around does not help us but hurt us. They prevent us from getting to that next level of life we are striving to attain. Breaking these ties are necessary for our life growth towards our true conscious calling.

Chapter 3:

WHAT ARE YOU DOING RIGHT NOW?
The Mindful Mind vs. The Thinking Mind

Take a moment to observe what you are doing this very minute. You are reading this book and what else? As you are reading, are you thinking about getting the car repaired, picking the children up from school, yesterdays office meeting that put more responsibilities on you, paying your bills this month, etc.? Or are you updating your status on Facebook? It is very easy to slip out of the mindful-mind and into the thinking mind. Being mindful involves bringing one's awareness back from the past or future, and into the present moment. The thinking mind is preoccupied with thoughts from the past or thoughts about the future. The thinking mind takes us out of the present moment, takes us out of reality, and puts us in a holding state. In order for us to live our true life, we must work on getting out of the thinking mind and moving into the mindful-mind.

Why is it important to be mindful?

Being mindful allows for constant awareness in all situations. When we are aware of our surroundings, we are able to experience them clearly and truthfully. We are no longer a spectator. Instead, we are active participants in life. When we are in the thinking mind, we are attached to our thoughts, our predisposed ideas, our past experiences, and the commentary that plays over and over in our minds. In the thinking mind, we have preconceived notions, make assumptions, make judgments, and place expectations on people and outcomes.

Mindfulness plays a central role in the teachings of the Buddha where it is affirmed that "correct" or "right" mindfulness is an essential factor in the path to enlightenment and liberation.

Being mindful makes us:

1. Aware of our surroundings
2. Experience life with clarity
3. A participant in life, not a spectator
4. Go beyond our preconceived thoughts and ideas

5. Go beyond our past experiences
6. Slow down and work to stop the constant commentary of the mind
7. Move past assumptions, judgments, and expectations and not let them interfere with what is currently taking place

How do we exit the thinking mind and enter into mindfulness?
There are several ways of doing this:

1. Breathing.
Mediation begins with being aware of your breathing. When we sit with our eyes partially closed (relax the eyes), we begin to move our attention to our breathing. Breathe naturally, preferably through the nostrils. Try to not control your breath; begin to become aware of the sensation of your breath as it flows in and out of the nostrils. The sensation of the breath is the objective of meditation. Concentrate on your breathing and block out everything else. In the beginning, our thoughts will try and distract us but with practice and observation of our thoughts, we can achieve clarity and mindfulness.

2. The way of the dog.

When we observe a dog, he is not bound by his preconceived thoughts, assumptions, judgments, or past experiences. He is in the present moment and actively participating in life. The older we become, the less interesting things seem to be. We tend to no longer enjoy activities like we used to. A dog looks at everything like the first time he is experiencing it. When we are able to enter the present moment, without the constant dialogue of the thinking mind, life is new and fun again, allowing you to truly enjoy every moment. You will truly know when you have done this successfully, because you will be happier, lighter, and more carefree with everything you do.

3. Music therapy.

When we use music to create mindfulness, we do this for both the calming and energizing effects music offers. When using music to create mindfulness we focus on the sounds and vibrations of each note or string we hear. When we are mindful with music, we observe the feelings the music creates within us and any other feelings and sensations that are happening in that moment.

4. Wash the dishes.

Instead of viewing the dishes as a mere chore, we must view it as a positive event. Eliminate the preconceived thoughts about doing the dishes and allow the experience to not be judged. As you wash the dishes, focus on washing the dishes and nothing more. When you are applying the soap to the dishes, feel the soap suds, feel the water temperature, and feel your fingers in the water. Get completely involved in the activity and in the moment. While you are washing the dishes, remember to keep your mind as clear as possible. When you begin to think of outsides thoughts, bring yourself back to the present moment and back to the dishes you are cleaning. The same can be done for cleaning the house. When we take away our preconceived thoughts and judgments, we make cleaning the house an exercise in clarity.

5. Driving your car.

We normally think of driving as a way from point A to B but it is much more. We can use driving as an exercise in mindfulness. When you get into your car, instead of racing to get somewhere, focus on the process. Some of us already use driving to clear our heads and this is exactly what I am referring to.

When we drive, we pay attention to driving, observing our surroundings, and being one with the vehicle. When driving around a curve, we feel ourselves being pushed in a certain direction within our seats. When we focus on driving, we hear the engine, feel the acceleration, feel the braking, and feel the wind or air conditioner in our hair and face. When we are at a traffic light, we notice the pedestrians walking across the street, we observe the traffic in front of us, behind, and side-to-side, and we begin to realize the calming effect of being mindful. If at anytime you catch thoughts creeping into your mind, observe them, let them go, and get yourself back to the present moment.

When we practice being mindful, we also practice observing our thoughts and letting them go. While participating in one of the above activities, we will catch ourselves thinking about something that happened earlier in the day or something we want to have happen in the future. See your thought, allow it to be, without placing value or judgment upon it, and let it go; then refocus back in the present moment. Sometimes laughing helps, so when you observe those thoughts creeping into the present moment, laugh as you acknowledge the thought, allow it to be, and then let it go.

When we practice being mindful, we allow ourselves to experience life with a renewed and more positive outlook. Being mindful frees us to be truer, happier, healthier, and more at peace with our surroundings and ourselves. When we are present in the moment, we begin to live our true life through active participation.

Personal reflection and Blog:

What music do you listen to that calms your mind and body?

What music do you listen to that energizes your mind and body?

What other activities are exercises in clarity for you?

Chapter 4:

EXPECTATIONS ARE OVERRATED

When we place expectations on outcomes, we place a high price on our happiness. Nothing is completely planned, if we are living in the present moment, we are not planning our future in a day planner and scratching things off as we go, we are living our life and loving every minute. So, stop planning! I'm not saying to stop making appointments or scheduling vacations, but stop placing expectations on everything you do. When we place expectations and specifications upon an event, we create a mind-formed event.

For example, when my spouse and I plan a vacation, we may go on line and find a destination and then find a hotel. While looking for a hotel, we might find a couple of places that seem to match us perfectly. After reading comments from other vacationers, we select one. We might also look at the pictures on the web site of the hotel and make our decision from there. If we get it in our heads that the hotel has to look a certain way and that the pictures have to be exact, then when we arrive at the hotel and things aren't exactly how they were in the pictures, we might get frustrated and upset with our destination and our trip. I realize, to a degree, our mind will form ideas and thoughts about a vacation, but we must make sure that our mind doesn't form strict expectations. When we place expectations and specifications upon anything in our lives, we can be disappointed.

Another example is the expectations we place upon our friends and family. We might expect them to act a certain way or to do a certain something, and when that doesn't happen, we feel let down. We will all get let down by others, but in reality it isn't others who let us down; we cause ourselves to be let down due to our expectations. Instead of expecting people to do things or to act a certain way, we must concentrate on ourselves, and what we should be doing. When we expect certain things from others, we can get hurt and disillusioned.

Because we are not in competition with others, we must continually work to better ourselves. It's not what others do; it's what we do, to better our surroundings and ourselves. Focus daily on making yourself better than you were yesterday. What others are doing is just that, what others are doing;

let them do what they need to do, and focus on your own growth and happiness.

Sometimes our expectations for others are based on the fact that we want them to do something that is in their own best interest. Even then, we must be careful. We must allow people to be themselves and allow them to make their own mistakes in life. If you allow others to make mistakes, and not take it personally when someone acts the opposite of what you thought they would, you will be in charge of your happiness.

With regards to best friends and family, the same applies. I agree that we should be able to depend on them, but remember, even if we depend on them to do something they said they would, don't get upset if they don't. It might be a cloudy day outside, it might not rain, but you might as well bring an umbrella just in case. With this analogy, I'm not saying to assume the worst, but to accept the unexpected and don't allow others' actions to take you off course. If someone fails to follow through with something, forgive it, forget it, and move on. If it happens often, I would suggest re-thinking your relationship with that person; most likely this is a rare occurrence. Just remember they are human and will make mistakes, but you don't have to let their mistakes effect you.

When we take a look at a normal day, our thinking mind can place many expectations on everything and everyone, setting us up for a day of unhappiness and disillusionment. It might begin as you are leaving for work in the morning, and continue all day long:

- You back out of the driveway and begin to drive down your street, you see a neighbor you know and wave and expect them to wave back and they don't.

- You arrive at work and see a friend of yours that you had a beer with the night before and you figure that you will probably have a funny conversation on the way into the building, nope, they give a wimpy hi and rush off. Before 9am you are 0 for 2!

- You get to your desk and begin working when you realize that you gave a co-worker a project to finish the night before and need that material, you call that person and it's not done and they aren't sure when it will be finished.

- Your spouse agreed last night that they would pick you up at your office and take you to lunch, but you receive a call from them twenty minutes before lunch telling you that they won't be making it because they are too busy.

You see where this is going. The more we expect, the more we get hurt emotionally. When we don't expect things, we don't get angry and upset when we don't receive specific outcomes. So lets begin our day again:

- We are pulling out of our driveway and begin driving down the street, you wave because you want to wave to your neighbor that is walking their dog. If they wave or don't wave, no problem, you did what you wanted to do and what makes you feel good.
- When you are entering the office you say hi to your friend you saw last night, that makes you feel good and that is who you are.

- When your spouse cancels lunch, fine, do something else.

Things do work out for a reason and if you follow your inner being, you will always be where you need to be, no matter what others do around you. For instance, the next time someone cancels on you at the last minute, think about it as a chance to do something else. When we begin to go with the life flow, we are suddenly open to all life has to offer.

I believe that when we eliminate expectations from our lives, we also rid our lives of some negativity, anger, resentment, and frustration. We can become negative because of things that happen that are out of our control and the mental spin we have placed upon those things. Aspects of our lives, which we can't control - like other people and their actions - shouldn't get us upset. Our lives become much easier and you become much happier because you are not always expecting a certain outcome. You become open to the moment and what is suppose to take place, not what you think you want or need at that very moment from that person or situation.

When we aren't expecting a certain outcome, we are able to take part in the present moment and appreciate what is taking place now, instead of using our present moment as a means to an end.

Eventually through practice, the placement of expectations on others will stop and you will feel at peace and have much more clarity toward yourself and your life. Expectations are something the mind developed to cause problems in our lives. It is better to be pleasantly surprised by one's actions then to be frustrated and hurt. The only person we should put expectations on is our self, and those expectations should be attainable.

Personal Reflection and Blog:

What events have you placed high expectations upon?
How did these particular events turn out?

With regards to people, whom do you place the highest expectations upon?
Why do you do this?

What personal work have you been doing to stop placing expectations on everything and everyone?

Chapter 5:

DO YOU LOVE YOURSELF?

Usually when we think about love, we think about the love between ourselves and another person. We might think of the love we have with our spouse, significant other, girlfriend or boyfriend. We might think of the love we have with our family, our mom, dad, grandmother, grandfather, etc. We may even think of the love we have with a dog, cat, or pet bird. The love we rarely think of is the love we have for ourselves. Self-love is mandatory to achieving your true life.

Why should we love ourselves?

1. To truly love another.
If we don't love ourselves, we can't truly love another. To truly love someone unconditionally, we must truly love ourselves unconditionally. Unconditional love is love that is given all the time no matter what and has no strings. True love is unconditional and places no perimeters or agility test on yourself or others to pass. When we truly love ourselves, we find ourselves in relationships

that supply and we supply back unconditional love. This love is not based on what another can do for you or what you can do for them; it is based on loving that person, no matter one's faults.

2. Life is challenging enough.
If you don't love yourself...Who will?
We can't expect another to truly love us if we can't love ourselves. Life is very challenging, much less going through it loathing one's self.

3. It allows for a good relationship with the person you're with 24/7. You! When we unconditionally love ourselves, we are able to be at peace and harmony with ourselves.

4. Inner harmony.
Self-acceptance is a wonderful thing because there is no battle going on inside of you to deal with on a daily basis. It's a lot easier to deal with what the world is handing you daily when you aren't battling yourself.

5. The company.
We find other people that love themselves as well, and that allows us to experience healthy relationships that benefit us, challenge us, and

add to our daily lives.

6. To make good and sound life choices.
When we love ourselves we are able to make good choices for ourselves. We choose to eat a certain way to stay healthy. We take care of our bodies by getting proper exercise, getting the right amount of sleep, getting timely medical checkups for prevention, and we use meditation tools to increase inner awareness and create our inner and outer balanced connection. When we love ourselves, we choose the way of healthy living to take care of our body so we have it for a long time.

How do we love ourselves?

1. Hush the internal critic.
Inside of us lurks an inner critic that is waiting to judge, sabotage, discount, critique, and have us question everything about ourselves. The critic is quick to take a good experience and begin to pick it apart and have us question if the experience was truly good. The critic is a ruthless judge that can judge everything about us, from our face, body, mind, actions, comments, work, projects, etc. Every time we look in the mirror, the critic has a chance to come out. If we allow it, the critic would

keep us home everyday because we would be too dissatisfied with ourselves to want to go out in public. This critic is a bully in a sense and needs to be stopped. The best way to stop the internal critic's dialogue is to be a witness to it. When we observe negative internal dialogue, observe it, and let it go. The first step of observation is paramount. Once you are able to observe your internal critic, you are then able to put a stop to those negative thoughts. Remember the critic is part of the thinking mind that's trying to hold us back.

2. Be a friend to yourself.
Treat yourself like you treat your friends. We all treat our friends with respect and love. When your friends are upset with themselves or having a problem, you show them love and support, so you must remember to show that same love and support to yourself. When we are friends to ourselves, we except and love everything about ourselves. Nurture all aspects of yourself, especially the ones that you don't particularly care for. When it comes to your body, love everything about it.

3. Deal with personal denial.
Denial is something we're all constantly dealing with and need to remove from our lives. In order to live

a healthy life, we must confront any denial that we still have in our lives. When we take an honest look at our lives, we can put some distance between the daily drama and our true self and really take a deep and clear look at our lives. What are the reoccurring issues we are dealing with? Do we have patterns in our lives? Do we have unhealthy patterns that we must stop? Are we denying issues/problems in our lives? Do we blame others for the things we do? Do you blame others for things that happen to you? Do we continue the same negative life patterns but constantly expect different outcomes and results? Confronting our personal denial can be difficult but it will make us stronger, wiser, healthier, and happier.

4. Connect with your core.
In order to connect with our core, we must remove the critic, deal with personal denial, and be our own friend. In order to maintain that healthy you, we must strengthen our connection with ourselves. In order to deepen that connection, we must do things for ourselves that bring us back to our core. Some people choose meditation, yoga, prayer, exercise, focusing on our breathing, practicing mindfulness, etc. When we get back to our core and accept ourselves for who we truly

are, we are more powerful, happier, healthier, and we can refocus that energy we were wasting on the inner critic and use that for other pursuits. Once we make that solid personal connection, we can never go back to not loving ourselves; we may have to constantly work at it, but we never forget it.

Ways to help us like ourselves and begin to love ourselves.

1. Choose your media intake wisely.
The media doesn't report on how to have a beautiful, happy, and healthy lifestyle. Recently, more programming are beginning to demonstrate healthy lifestyles, but for the most part, we are surrounded by negative and unhealthy media that doesn't support a healthy self-image. The media tends to glamorize and demonstrate the unhealthy and unhappy, instead of the positive and well-balanced lifestyle. With that said, we can feel good and look good but don't need to obsess. Rather than obsessing over getting older and/or gaining weight, you must do what's best for your body and concentrate on your health. Try to stay young inside and out by eating well and taking good care of you. If you want to get procedures done at the doctor's office to take a few years off your face,

do it, but don't do it for anyone else but yourself. In the end, it is you that has to live with you and because of that, only do what you want to do. Whatever you choose, you must be happy and comfortable with yourself.

2. Care about your health.

When we care about our health, we care about ourselves. Only you can take care of yourself and make sure that you are healthy and performing at your best level. This requires seeing your doctor regularly and following up with any regiments you need to be doing to keep yourself healthy. Exercising is also important to maintain a healthy and happy body. When we exercise, our bodies show us thanks by building muscle and having a happier and healthier outlook. Exercise not only helps your body but also helps your mind. When we exercise our body produces endorphins that make us feel good. Regular exercise helps our bodies maintain good blood pressure, muscle tone, and a healthy emotional state. Selecting a workout regimen that you follow is very important for your overall health and wellbeing. Hiring a personal trainer is a good option for learning correct workout techniques and for quick adaptation to a good workout regimen that your body will respond positively to. Besides working out and seeing your doctor regularly, you must also take an active role as chief nutritionist for yourself.

Your body needs the correct foods and supplements to allow it to perform at its best. You can begin by seeing a nutritionist and figuring out the foods that help you and the foods that hurt you. You can visit the bookstore or go on line and do research for the best foods for your blood type. You are the best person to determine what foods are best for you. Our bodies need vegetables, proteins, carbohydrates, etc to thrive. With that in mind, determine what your body likes and doesn't like to eat and process. Our bodies are all wired differently, because of that we can digest certain foods better than others. When someone is lactose intolerant, they need extra enzymes to process and breakdown certain dairy sugars. There are enzymes that help breakdown fats, carbohydrates, protein, and fiber. While you are researching proper nutrition, also look into the best vitamins and supplements to better your body. When we speak about vitamins, we must begin with the multivitamin. Choosing a multivitamin is not difficult; you need to select one for your gender and be sure it is comprehensive. I find that taking a multivitamin that contains the entire dosage in one or two pills is best. It's less harsh on the stomach and costs less. You determine if you prefer it in a liquid or pill form. Besides multivitamins, there are supplements for building the immune system. Our bodies need these supplements; because they help ~~our bodies~~ fight disease everyday. There are many mushroom-based supplements that help support the immune system, the cardiovascular system, and provide reinforcement for the immune system and your entire body. These types of supplements are rarely found in a multivitamin. There are several brands of supplements on the market. The important thing is to find supplements that are organic. The best are the 100% vegetarian supplements with no coloring, no binders, and no flavorings. Other supplements that you might want to add to your daily health routine would be vitamin D, flax seed oil, and elderberry. Besides pill form supplements, getting your proper daily protein amount is also very important. There are many different types of protein powder on the market. They are whey, soy, or rice protein. Many studies have been done on what protein is right for men and women. Finding a good one is based upon protein amount, vitamin composition, and good taste. There are many on the market that provides proper protein, vitamins, and minerals. Last but not least, remember to drink the proper amount of water. Water is essential to a healthy body. When we take an active role with our health and bodies by eating healthy, taking proper supplements, vitamins, and exercising, we are actively living life.

3. Observe, evaluate, change or delete the negative influences in your life.

Do you have any outside influences that are negatively influencing your life? Can you identify them? How are they negatively influencing you? Why are you allowing that around you? Media can be a negative influence and can come in the form of news programming, violence-depicting programming, argumentative programming, and even the 'non-sense' programming, that doesn't add to the quality of life. When I turn on the television, there are many programming options but many of them are filled with violence, drama, and negativity. When you watch television, choose wisely what you view and allow into your life.

Negative influences can also come in the form of a person. If a person in your life is constantly putting you down, hurting your feelings, and/or disappointing you, you must observe and evaluate why you are allowing this into your life. Once we have observed and are aware of the situation, we must first work on changing the situation. Changing the situation begins with changing how we react to what they say, do, or not do. Because we don't control others, we can't control how they act, what they do, and what they say. With that in mind, instead of trying to change their actions, reactions, and comments, we can change how we physically and emotionally react toward them. In these situations, we must protect and take care of ourselves. We can do this by setting reasonable and responsible personal boundaries.

If every time you watch that certain program on television, you leave it feeling angry, upset, or depressed, observe why it makes you feel that way. Once you have observed why it makes you feel a certain way, and you understand why it triggers these emotions, then you can work on stopping its effect on you. If conscious observation doesn't stop these negative emotions, then I would advocate stopping the viewing of these programs and filling your time with beauty instead of the negative. The same with regards to others, if every time you are around a particular person, you feel inadequate, sad, and/or upset, identify how that person is making you feel. Once you have identified the reason for your feelings, that person should not be able to make you feel inadequate or upset anymore. If you are still feeling that way, maybe it's time to spend less time with that person.

4. Sometimes, put yourself first.

Most of the time we are more concerned with everyone beside ourselves. Sometimes you have to put you first. For anyone that has ever flown on an airplane, you know that before take off, a flight attendant stands up, at the front of the aisle, and goes through the safety measures for the flight. One of the safety matters they cover is if there is a loss in cabin pressure, air masks will deploy from the ceiling. What they say next is important, secure the oxygen mask on yourself, and then secure the mask on the child or person seated next to you. If the mask isn't properly secure on you, you aren't going to be able to help the person next to you. This situation pertains to many facets of life. If you are run down, sick, depressed, etc., you can't help anyone else. Taking care of you and putting yourself first is not a bad thing, it's a necessity.

5. Spend time enjoying you.

When we spend time just for ourselves, we get to know ourselves better. However, instead of spending

EXCELLENT - AN ANALOGY

time with ourselves, we tend to want to spend it with as many other people as possible. Most of us are very social beings and want to be around people often if not all of the time. After work and even during the work hours, we begin making plans for the evening with our friends. When the workday is over, we race home to get ready to go out that night. We can do that over and over and the only time we stay home is when we are physically sick, tired of going out, or have a big meeting in the morning and know if we go out we'll miss it. Going out with friends can be fun but so is spending time with you. Instead of waiting until you are sick to spend time with yourself, begin now by planning a night for you. If you like movies choose or rent a movie you want to watch, buy some dinner, or prepare dinner, and try not to think about what everyone else is doing and what you might be missing out on. When I first tried this, I felt like I was always missing something, but quickly, I realized that I wasn't missing anything. When I began working on "my time", I paid too much attention to my phone. It took a lot of willpower to not answer it but I did it. After a little practice, spending time with me became fun and easier. Eventually, I would leave my phone in another room and not wonder who was calling me or what they were doing. By spending quality time with you, you develop a true sense of self and ultimately realize self-love. When we love ourselves, we take care of ourselves and make time for ourselves. Even if you are married you can still make time for yourself. You can plan activities that you like to do and do them with just you. It is good to have some time for you; it allows you to recharge your batteries. When you have children, it can be a little trickier, but your personal time has never been more important. In order to be a good and healthy parent, you must find time for you. Whether you go to a movie, fix yourself a meal, or drive a few miles out of town and look at the stars, whatever it is you choose to spend your time doing, do it right and for that given time, focus on what you are doing and focus on you. When you are watching the movie allow yourself to laugh and cry out loud. When you are eating, don't rush through the meal, take your time and enjoy it. If you are looking at the stars, take your time, allow the sky to fill you up, and allow yourself this time and this experience to revitalize you.

When we begin to fully love ourselves, we are happy, healthy, beautiful, and wise people. Half of life's battle is over, because we have ended the battle with ourselves. Wherever you go, you will project a wonderful feeling that others will catch on to. You will be at peace with yourself and more at peace with your surroundings. When you love yourself, you allow you to be you. Every relationship needs time, energy, and love. You can't be friends with someone unless you get to know them. You can't love someone unless you spend time with him or her. The same goes for yourself, you have to spend time with you to be your true friend and to love yourself.

Personal Reflection and Blog:

Have you been working on your friendship with yourself?

What have you been doing daily to nurture the important relationship with yourself?

What are you doing now to take better care of yourself?

How many times a week are you exercising?
Have you seen a change in your energy level?
Have you seen a change in your emotional level and general attitude toward life?

Personal Reflection and Blog: (continued)

What are some observations you have made of your internal critic?

Where do these internal negative thoughts come from?

What are you currently doing to rid yourself of these thoughts and replace them with positive, life supporting thoughts?

LIVE YOUR TRUE LIFE

Chapter 6:

BE YOURSELF
AND BY THE WAY, WHO ARE YOU?

When you know who you are, you act accordingly? When you don't understand yourself you can't begin to understand others. Who are you and why do you categorize yourself as so? What makes you laugh, smile, and cry? What makes you, you? When evaluating these questions, we must allow internal insight to play a large part in putting the puzzle pieces together. Because we all come from the same source, we aren't completely different from anyone else. We can identify the pieces of ourselves that we see in others. When we meet people, we can develop connections quickly when we are of similar nature and have some of the same qualities. On the other hand, it might be more difficult to establish a friendship or understanding with someone that appears to be opposite or different from us. With that in mind however, we can learn from everyone we meet. Everyone has something to teach us and everyone has something to learn.

What makes you a unique individual?

1. Values. Our values make us unique because our values define our motives for our actions and our way of life. Values are those things that really matter to each of us. What do we value? What do we place absolute no value upon? A personal code of values defines that which is important to you; not something you want or would like to have, but something you need in your life to live truly. Values are personal and because they are personal, they are different for all. When we think of things we value, we tend to think of life, animals, people, the environment, etc. We use our personal values to determine our actions. For example: if we value animals and their rights, we're not going to do anything that would harm an animal, and we might donate monetary funds to organizations like the SPCA or PETA. We might go a step further and donate our time and talent to these organizations. When we are driving down a street and see a homeless animal, we will stop and see if we can help the animal.

2. Theories. Our theories on life and why we are here make us unique. Many of us have various theories on why we are here and who put us here,

and those theories are very individual and very important to each person. Over time, we have put together these theories through our experiences, reasoning, and education. The most wonderful aspect about a theory is that a theory can be changed at any time to accommodate new information or new knowledge you acquire on the subject.

3. Beliefs. Our individual beliefs are just as unique as each of us. When we believe in something, we hold a thought or opinion in high regard based on experience and or evidence. If we didn't have the ability to believe, we would not be able to relate fully to other people, places, or things. Because we have the ability to believe, we are able to grasp and understand other things even when we haven't experienced them. When we believe something, we can relate to it.

4. Experiences. Our experiences are unique, which allows us to see the world differently than others see the world. Some of our experiences can be life changing and make us reevaluate our theories, beliefs, and values. It's not until we realize another's experiences that we are able to understand why a person acts a certain way. Our experiences have molded us into the people we

are today. For example: If we've never had a dog as a pet, we would not understand why having a dog is such a joyful experience. Also because of not having a dog, we wouldn't understand what it's like to lose a dog to a terminal illness. Without ever having a dog, a person wouldn't ever experience the emotions that come with the love and the death of the pet. We can imagine what it feels like and try to comfort the person that's experiencing the loss, but we haven't truly experienced it for ourselves. We've all tried to explain an experience we've had to someone and they couldn't fathom what we were trying to explain. Sometimes, people truly want to understand what you've been through but until they have truly experienced it, they can't. Some of us have experienced what we would like to call a miracle and after experiencing this miracle, it would be impossible to not believe in a higher power. Most of us that have experienced something in that regard have tried to share it with others and received mixed reviews. Some of the people you shared this with tried to understand and believed you and maybe had an experience of their own, but there were others that didn't understand and questioned you. Unfortunately, in this situation, instead of inspiring and enlightening others with your experience, you were reversed into defending yourself and trying to prove what you experienced. Unfortunately, as a result we may place ourselves only around people with similar life experiences that limit our ability to gain a broader perspective on life.

5. Past. Our past feeds directly into our experiences. The past that we have experienced and lived through, truly places its mark on our present attitude, our lifestyle, our choices, and our actions. All of us have different pasts and we've all experienced hardships; with that in mind, we cannot judge another for what they do. Instead we might try and understand why someone picks a certain life path and what might have prompted him or her to do so. Our past dictates so much of who we are today. We can definitely recount past experiences and learn from them but we must remember that the past is the past; we shouldn't wallow in it or hide there. Nor should we try and forget or lie about our past. If you feel ashamed of your past, you must allow the past to be and move on to the present before you miss it. When we live in the past, we miss the present entirely.

6. Present. Living our life in the present tense is so important. Our past experiences can cloud our actions and judgments. Sometimes, it is necessary to use past events to shed light on present situations, but we can't act out of fear when dealing with the present. The present allows us to make all changes we need in order to have a true life that allows for our happiness, progress, and daily self-improvement. All we have is the present moment, we can't go back and change the past, we must focus on the moment we have, and create what we need for ourselves. In the present, all things can be changed for the better. The present is the present, anything can happen in this moment. Lets not confuse the present with the future. The present moment we have is truly a gift. We can choose to appreciate it and go with the flow and not against it. We can choose to look back and concentrate on the past or look beyond it and dream up a possible future. In order to live truly, we must live in the moment, have our past for the memories and the learning curve, and focus on the present and make the best out of this moment that we've been given. The past is the past and realizing that means we can't go back and change events but we can make things right now in the present moment.

7. Environment. Our environment definitely impacts our thoughts and emotions. When our environment is peaceful, we are able to feel safe and not threatened. We can focus on other pursuits and not worry or be controlled by fear. However, sometimes we can't change our environment, and we must learn to live within it and thrive. In order to do that, we must see the positive in our environment and not dwell upon fear. Because our environment shapes us so much personally, we must strive to better our environment anyway we can. Whether we help with city programs for children or animals, pick up trash we see on the streets and sidewalks, help a lost person with directions, give a sandwich to a homeless person, recycle ~~our waste,~~ be an active participant in crime watch programs for the community, carpool, etc, we can all find ways to make our environment better for everyone. Living in a peaceful and clean environment is necessary to improve our quality of life, and we can all do our part to supply that.

8. Friends. The friends we select have a huge impact on our lives, theories, beliefs, experiences, and the present moment. A good friend helps us become wiser, gives us constructive criticism, and provides sound and unbiased advice. We need

friends who care about the things we care about and care about us. Friends must also share your commitment to truth, growth, and love. A friend must have your best interests at heart and you for them. Our friends help to color and vitalize our lives. When our friends are mindful and living truly, we are able to thrive in a positive and growth driven environment.

9. Family. Family is an essential part of our lives. As a child, our parents shaped our environment and instilled certain values in us, much as their parents did for them. For instance, if you had parents or grandparents that lived during the Great Depression, they generally live very conservatively with regards to money and material items, knowing the value of a dollar and a hard day's work. Our families past experiences shape our lives forever, and we should strive to learn from their triumphs and mistakes.

What about emotions?

We all have a theory on why we are here. I have a theory on why I am here and who put me here and I am happy with that theory at this time. I act accordingly to that theory by living my life in a positive manner and helping the people around me grow and thrive. I try to always love unconditionally and realize that I too make mistakes, and if I can't forgive someone for making a mistake, I'm making an even worse mistake, because I'm allowing their mistake to get in the way of my love for them. All the wonderful things that come from loving another are gone when we identify a person with their mistakes in the past. When we begin to judge others by their faults, we begin to put up walls and barriers between love and us.

With regards to emotions, there are only two emotions we as humans can have toward anyone or anything. Those two emotions are love and fear all other emotions are sub-categorical that feed off of the two.

Love has many sub-categorical emotions, for example Joy, Peacefulness, happiness, forgiveness, completeness, inspiration, harmony, playfulness, … there are too many to list. When we choose love we are living in the moment, not living in the past, and not allowing the thinking mind to take over. On the other end of the emotional spectrum, fear is the most basic and most powerful human emotion.

Fear has many sub-categorical emotions:
1. Hate
2. Paranoia
3. Guilt
4. Inadequacy
5. Discontent
6. Prejudice
7. Anger
8. Resentment
9. ...

How do we create love, and not fear, in our lives?

1. Choose it. It's that easy. When we choose love we get love. We can choose our own emotions; no one can choose them for us.

2. Make your decision. Albert Einstein said, "The single most important decision any of us will ever make is whether or not to believe the universe is friendly." Do you look at the universe as a loving place or are you fearful of it? If we believe the world is a fearful place, we will see only the negative in the world. If we see the world as a loving place, we will see the love the world has to offer, and so we will not fear the world. Fear can make us feel backed into a

corner, afraid that something bad will happen to us. When we choose love, we choose to not be a victim of fear, and to not be bullied by it.

3. Identify with it. When you identify with an emotion you can begin to see that emotion within you. In order to love, we must realize that we are love. Love is abundance and not scarcity. When we lead with love, we are sharing and working in cooperation with others. When we lead with fear, we offer selfishness because we aren't sharing or promoting cooperation. All of the fear-based emotions are very empty and emotionally draining. When we work from a scarcity principle, we never have enough and we are always fearful that we will soon run out. When we are fearful, we cut ourselves off from others and are alone.

4. Don't live in the thinking mind. Our minds can make us see things in the worst light. The mind can play tricks on us and create havoc in our lives. When we live in the thinking mind and not in the present moment, we can associate fear with anything. We can over think something and create barriers in our mind. When we live in the moment, we are able to experience the moment for what it is and not allow preconceived notions, which often breed fear,

to sabotage the moment. In life, we can self-sabotage by listening to the thinking mind and not allowing for spiritual, mental, and emotional growth.

5. When all else fails, look in the mirror and smile. When you are feeling down and nothing seems to take you out of that feeling, go to a well-lit mirror and smile as big as you can. Look into the mirror and observe you and your smile. Keep smiling and be in the present moment. After smiling for a short period of time, you will begin to feel emotionally lifted. Continue to smile until you are genuinely smiling and continue to stay in the moment.

Once you have established love as your chosen emotion, you can begin to take on an even more powerful and strengthened role in life; this is a role that you deserve and need in order to live your true life.

Personal Reflection and Blog:

What do you value the most in life?
Do your actions and words display to others and yourself what you value?
If not, do you think you should rethink your actions or your true values?

Personal Reflection and Blog: (continued)

Is there a possibility that your core values have changed?

Are you working to eliminate fear in your life?

What are the changes you are making to create a more loving environment for yourself and others?

Which life experiences have really shaped your life? In what way have these experiences shaped your life?
Have you learned from them?
Have you learned more about yourself through these experiences?
Are there any past experiences that weren't pleasant but you wouldn't change even if you could, because you truly grew from the experiences?

What do you look for in a true friend?

What do you offer a true friend?
Are you surrounded by people that love, care, and value your friendship?
If not, what changes and personal choices do you feel you need to make in order to have and embrace a quality friend base?

Chapter 7:

TIME TRAVEL, DO YOU HAVE A TIME MACHINE?

In the recent film, Harry Potter and the Prisoner of Azkaban, two children by the names of Harry Potter and Hermione Granger have the option, with the help of a magical "time turner", to go back in time and save two lives, thereby changing the course of history. In the movie, they successfully go back in time and accomplish what needs to be done. All of us at one time or another would love to turn back the hands of time and re-do something we didn't do well or failed to do. Unfortunately, in real life there are no do-overs.

Turning back the clock is impossible at this time. Unfortunately, many of us don't live our life with that in mind. We tend to live our lives with a certain disregard – a lack of thoughtfulness - sometimes resulting in a failure to follow through for others and for ourselves.

When we fail to follow through for others, we have a tendency to lose friends, make enemies, or just fall out of favor. Sometimes, we get labeled the hack, the ditz, and the talker that no one listens to anymore. When you keep promising and never deliver, you create problems in your life.

When we fail to follow through with promises to ourselves, we create stagnation and despair. If we keep promising ourselves that we will enroll in a class, take a trip, or take better care of ourselves and we never follow through, we eventually lose the drive to better ourselves.

Because we don't possess a time turner to go back in time and better our wrongdoings and missed chances, we must be mindful participants in life. Being a mindful active participant in life means that on a daily basis we must focus on our dreams, pursuits, aspirations, making a difference, striving to love in a more unconditional way, choosing love over fear, not living in the thinking mind, not placing expectations on everything and everyone, and living in the present moment and being an active participant not a spectator.

How to live without the need for time travel

1. Focus on your dreams, pursuits, and aspirations. Everyone's day is busy with a multitude of deadlines and responsibilities. Because of these daily responsibilities, it makes it difficult and sometimes impossible to focus on our goals. For your own happiness, it is important to secure a few minutes a day to focus on your goals and what you need to achieve them. All of us have looked up one day and realized that we are getting older and we haven't attained our goals yet. That feeling is an empty one that leaves us with sad thoughts and feelings of scarcity and depression. Let's stop that by considering our goals daily. Let's begin by getting a legal pad or notebook and on the first page, write down what it is you want to accomplish in your life. Underneath the written-out goal or goals, write why you want to accomplish this goal. Basically, why is achieving this goal important to you? After you have considered this and written your reason or reasons underneath, tear the page out of your notebook and hang it somewhere you will see it every day. If you can remember to take the notebook with you daily, then leave the page attached and consult it daily. Next, turn the page and write down the resources, skills, knowledge, and materials that you already

possess that will help you achieve your goal. After you have done that, turn the page and write what it is that you can do to get closer to achieving your goal. Can you do some research on the internet, call and speak to others that are doing what you want to be doing, go to the library and check out some books on the subject, etc.

By making these well-organized lists, we are able to reflect on the things we have and the things we need to get closer to achieving our goal. Write a list of things that you can do to get closer to achieving that goal. Next, turn the page and write down what things you need to possess to obtain that goal. For example: if you want to get into television acting. You will need to have acting lessons. If you've already taken several classes, those classes will go on the previous page where you have listed your skills and knowledge that you already possess. If you are looking into entering commercial work, and you haven't taken acting for commercials, that particular class will go on this page, the page of things that need to be accomplished. The following page should be contacts you have that can help you achieve this goal. If you have friends, families, or acquaintances that are involved in this business or who know someone in the business, list them on this page. When you list these people, put down as much contact information as you have for each individual. Going back to our acting example, you might want to get an acting coach to better your success. On this list, you might know an acting coach or have a friend that has used an acting coach. After making contact with that person and you have made an appointment with an acting coach, you are that closer to achieving your goal. Through the coach and others that are in the industry you will find a photographer for your headshots and an agent when the time comes. Otherwise, if you don't know anyone that is an acting coach or has used one, reflect back to the list of things needed to research and add that one to the list. You could go online and find acting coaches in your area and read up on them. You could also visit them and 'interview' them to see if you will work well together. These lists help because they allow you to not feel overwhelmed with all the things that need to be done in order to obtain your goal. When we just dream about what we want in our lives and not map out our course of action, we become overwhelmed and less likely to achieving it. By making these well-organized lists, we are able to reflect on the things we have and the things we need to get closer to achieving our goal. Because you are going about achieving your goal in an organized and deliberate manner, you will feel more fulfilled and begin to realize your goal as a reality and not feel overwhelmed. When we just think about what we want without trying to achieve it, we never get near it. We always wonder if we could have done it. Would we have been great? Instead, when we create a clear pathway to get there, we are realistically trying to achieve something. When we deliberately work toward our goals we learn about ourselves and we are more likely to be successful in achieving them. Remember that the journey to achieving your goal is the most important aspect of achieving the goal. Don't overlook the journey. Throughout the journey you will learn things about yourself, others, and the universe that you didn't realize before. Remember as you proceed through your journey to always be mindful and in the present moment. The journey is not just a means to an end; love every minute of it. Remember to laugh and have fun, its part of the journey.

2. Make a difference. Achieving your own goal is important but so is making a difference in this world. Everyday we need to focus on making a difference within our society and our environment. Being kind and considerate to others we come into contact with is a start to making a difference in this world. We

don't have a time turner and because of that, we must act accordingly. We can't take things back that we say or do and because of that, we must say and do the right things by all.

When we are polite and truthful to all, we do the right thing by being the best person we can be. This is as simple as opening a door for someone, letting someone into your lane on the highway, helping someone with directions, or giving some money or some food to a homeless individual. All of these actions count more than we think.

If we are taking a walk and we see newspaper or trash on the sidewalk, we should pick it up and throw it away. If we see a lost or homeless animal about to walk through a busy intersection, try and help that animal.

When we have conversations with others, remember that what you say is important. If you are angry about something, think before you speak because nothing can be completely taken back. Also, telling people how you feel about them is important. If you love them, tell them you love them. When my father lost his father, he didn't get a chance to tell him he loved him and it has affected him his entire life.

Always say what needs to be said. It's easier to say something instead of thinking about and not doing it. I tell everyone I care about that I care about them, love them, etc. You don't get a second chance. Life is unpredictable and because of that unpredictability, it is imperative to let others know your feelings, thoughts, etc. Remember when you give respect, you get respect.

3. Choose love over fear. Loving unconditionally is something that everyone can work on. Loving completely unconditionally is difficult for most but should be something we constantly aim toward. When we truly love, we don't allow people's mistakes to get in the way of our love. When we truly love someone, we must look beyond their faults and love them for them. Loving without condition placement is a Godly attribute but has to be worked on and cultivated. Most of us love our friends no matter what they do. It seems easier to love our friends more unconditionally then our family, spouse, or children, but we must try to do the same. It seems we place more standards and conditions on the closest people in our lives. The more we love unconditionally the less we are hurt by others' actions or inactions. We must allow others to be themselves and not impose our

restrictions and demands upon them.

In the same way, we must love ourselves unconditionally and not find constant fault. We must be able to forgive others and ourselves when mistakes are made. I believe that we are the hardest on ourselves and because of that we put high standards on others. Everyone is human and to be human is to make mistakes. With that in mind, we must place fewer conditions on the ones we love. For example: If you have a dog, and the dog relieves himself on the carpet, you initially tell him not to do that, you clean it up, and move on. You don't love the dog any less because he made a mistake. So why do we allow others' mistakes to get in the way of our feelings for them?

When we choose love over fear our lives get better, happier, and easier. The world seems to be a friendlier place and dealing with the day-to-day issues aren't struggles anymore. When we choose love, we choose to accept people, and we reap the benefits of being whole and happy. Everything around us might not be perfect but we must not focus on the things that aren't perfect, we must focus on the things that are going right in our lives.

With regards to the things that we feel aren't perfect, we must ask ourselves "what is perfection?" Why are we striving for perfection? Is there true perfection with regards to anything? Is the idea of perfection just another way to get us farther away from whom we truly are, to find drama and unhappiness instead of peacefulness, and to ultimately find fault in others and ourselves? Instead of focusing on imperfections that are mind cultivated, we choose to love; we choose to be loving, and generous to all. Being loving and generous is much easier than being fearful and angry all the time. When we love and are positive even our health seems to get better, we are more relaxed and easy going. When we stop placing conditions and expectations on others, we begin to enjoy life more. These conditions and expectations are attributes of the thinking mind and do not allow us to be mindful and present. To choose love over fear is to be mindful because we are not acting from a scarcity principle and we aren't acting on our mind based thoughts that can manipulate any situation into being a negative one. The present moment is a gift, be thankful for it and allow it to be. Don't make the present a means to an end; the present is all we have, the future has yet to be determined. However, if we are the best person we can be in the present moment, our future will definitely be brighter, happier, richer, and filled with much love.

4. Stop living in the thinking mind. We can begin by not placing expectations on everything and everyone; then we will start to live in the present moment, and we become a life participant, not just a spectator.

When we spend our time in the thinking mind, we spend less time in the present moment. You can't be in multiple places at once, so what's more important? The present moment is most important because that is what is taking place now. We've all experienced being in one situation, but all we could think about is something that took place earlier. When we go back into the thinking mind and remove ourselves from the moment, we are removing ourselves from life.

For example, when we get together with old friends, it's lots of fun, but sometimes we can just focus on our old stories and situations. That is fun to talk about but after a while, if that's all you do, you haven't developed the friendship any further. The friendship has stagnated and you begin to realize that maybe all that you and that other person have is the past. Sometimes, old friendships can be revitalized and allowed to grow and change; other times, old friendships are just that, old friendships. You are still friends but the friendship can't grow and progress. Talking about the old stories is just that, talking about the old stories. When we are thinking about the past, we are not growing or progressing, and we aren't even participating in life. If you can't get past the past and grow and mature together in the moment, there's only stagnation and a misuse of time.

Sometimes when you leave people, after you talked about old stories, you realize that you don't know any more about that person then you did before. It also leaves you with an empty feeling, because you didn't take anything from that meeting; much like when we live in the mind and not participate in the moment, we are missing out on life and creating an empty feeling. It's much like the idea of not being happy where you are and always looking elsewhere for the bigger better deal. Some people are never happy where they are. If you catch yourself wanting to jump place to place, you must realize that you are no longer in the moment. You are back in the thinking mind and are not allowing this moment to be. Being in the moment and being aware of life and your position in it allows for true happiness and peace. When we are truly in the moment, we are happy, content, and actively participating in life.

Since we don't have a time turner, we must take advantage of each moment we are given. We can't get the last five minutes back, nor can we get back the last five years, so we must make the most of the present. When we are actively participating and focusing on the moment at hand, we are making the most of it.

Next time you catch yourself not being present in the moment, remember that you don't have a time turner and can't bring back the time you have lost. Instead of dwelling on lost time, refocus on the moment, be mindful, and jump back into life, don't let it pass you by! When we live in the mind, we might as well go home, take no phone calls, and cut ourselves off from society, because we aren't participating in life. The thinking mind puts up barriers between yourself and others, and the present moment can't penetrate it without us stepping in, observing the thinking mind, letting those thoughts go, and getting back into the moment we've been given.

Personal Reflection and Blog:

When was the last time you caught yourself not in the moment? What were you thinking about?

At what point did you begin to observe the thinking mind? Where you out with friends? Driving your car? At work?

Have you caught yourself placing expectations on people or situations? What were the expectations? What was the outcome?

Can you tell a difference in your life participation when you are being mindful instead of being in the thinking mind?

Do you feel that when you are out of the thinking mind, that you are able to be where you need to be when you need to be there? (Important)

Chapter 8:

YOU ARE WHAT YOU EAT
YOU ARE WHAT YOU SEE AND HEAR

We have one mind and in that mind, there are two sections. They are the conscious and the subconscious. Many view the subconscious as the source of creativity, strength, inventiveness, etc. The conscious mind makes up a small part of the mind in comparison to the subconscious mind. If you think of your mind in terms of a computer, the images and content on the screen is your conscious mind and everything on your hard drive is your subconscious mind. Everything that we see and hear gets stored in our subconscious mind. These things that are stored can either benefit, or detract from, our minds and our lives.

Our senses are bombarded daily with information from many media sources. We can't always choose what we are exposed to, but most of the time we can. What you allow yourself to view and listen to, are very important choices that should be made wisely. We sometimes give little thought to the music we listen to and the television programs and films we watch. Our minds are very absorbent and tend to cling to things that we see and hear. Even if you aren't paying attention to something on the television or the radio, your subconscious mind always is. Our brains never stop working; they pick up everything and keep it in our subconscious. Scientists have learned that our subconscious stores everything we come into contact with; it controls much of what we do and how we feel and act, and it contains the knowledge and thoughts that drive us to do what we do and feel how we feel. That's why, in our spare time, what we allow ourselves to view and listen to are very important selections and should be chosen wisely.

When you listen to the radio, your brain is picking up on all the lyrics of the songs, so if the songs you are listening to are violent and negative in nature, your thoughts will be as well. If you are watching violent television programs and films, these violent thoughts will seep into your mind and contaminate your thoughts and feelings. Negative images and thoughts can reside inside the subconscious mind and in order to remove them we must fill the mind with the positive instead of the negative.

Lets think of the mind as a glass of water, this glass of water may have some clean drinkable water inside of it but some of it might be murky and discolored. With a glass of water, it's easy enough to empty the glass in the sink, wash it really well, and refill it with clean water. Our subconscious minds are a bit more challenging to "clean." Think of the subconscious mind as the glass of water, but this glass of water is affixed to the table, and because you can't move it to empty the murky water, you must bombard the glass with clean water so that the murky water flows out and the glass now contains good healthy water.

We've all heard people talk about how negative the news seems to be and so I decided to do a test of my own. For several days in a row, I sat on the couch and watched news the entire day. After the first day, my husband came home and kept asking me if I was all right. I assured him I was and kept watching the news; after a while, I was definitely depressed, felt sluggish, felt nothing I did in this world really matters, and I wondered if their was any good news in the world. It's amazing what our mind does when we bombard it with negative images.

The great thing about this feature of our mind is that when we fill it with positive thoughts and images, we can't stay upset or depressed, instead we fill elevated and invigorated.

How do we cleanse our subconscious mind?

1. Don't leave the television or radio on when going to sleep. The problem with leaving one of these devices on is that eventually you do go to sleep and anything can be invading your mind. It's like having no guard at the castle. When you are asleep and these things are entering your mind, you have no defense to it. Instead of using the radio or television as a tool to help you sleep, read a book or try focusing on your breathing and or practice meditation.

2. When you are watching or listening to something, pay attention to your heart rate and breathing. Sometimes the best notification of what we need to be watching or listening to comes to us in the form of what our bodies are doing while exposed to these stimuli. When you are paying attention to your heart rate and breathing, you are also paying attention to yourself and not giving all of your attention and energy to an outside stimulus, thereby monitoring your intake of said stimuli.

3. When watching television, take breaks and remember to get up and move around. After one hour of television, it is best to move around, get up, and do something different. The worse thing is to sit there and be a part of a television marathon. In order to be consciously paying attention to your body and how you are feeling, you must get the blood flowing. We've all heard someone say, "I'm vegging out watching television." That is completely true. When someone is vegging out, they are not thinking for themselves. Television can be used for entertainment and education but must be regulated and self-monitored.

4. Try less television or no television at all. Television time should be limited. Just like anything else, television viewing should be done in moderation. When you don't overindulge, you limit the negative impact. When we choose to watch television, we must also make correct choices on the programming and the time limitation. Many people tell me that after they have stopped watching television for a few days, they are more creative, have a better outlook on life, and are more productive throughout their day.

5. Use a DVR. Often TV viewing can be analogous to eating ice cream from the carton – once you start you never know how much you have eaten, so you are less likely to limit your intake to a pre-desired level. If you are going to watch TV, I suggest you take advantage of the benefits of a DVR and only watch those particular programs you record. This is also a great way to avoid the negativity and manipulation of advertising – just zip right thru it! This saves you about 25% of your viewing time also. If you taped two shows, watch one show and in-between, get up and move around, fix something to eat, or take a walk, then watch the other show. After that show is finished, turn off the television and move on to another activity.

6. Music is a powerful stimulus. Music has the ability to lift us up or put us down. There are neural correlations to the often-powerful emotional responses to music. Many studies have been performed with regards to the effects of music on our bodies. Doctors have played "sad" excerpts of music for patients and found lower heart rate, blood pressure, skin conductance and temperature. They have played "fearful" music excerpts and those produced increases in heart rate and blood pressure. The "happy" excerpts produced the largest changes

in the measures of respiration.

Positive affirmations, as referenced in Chapter 2 can also be found within a song. If you find a song that talks about where you want to be and how you want to see yourself, listening to that over and over again is not a bad idea. We all realize that when we listen to music, even if we aren't trying to, we can quickly pick up on the lyrics and possibly begin singing along. Because of this ability, the music we listen to needs to be based upon positive things that we are wanting in our subconscious minds.

Violence on television and in film does not help us to grow. We have child proofing for the television and the internet, but we don't have adult proofing for ourselves. Each of us needs to instill our own proofing system that protects our easily absorbent mind from the negativity and violence in our media. In order to be healthy and happy people, we must help ourselves and keep ourselves away from harmful material.

The content on TV seems to be dominated by negativity. For instance, the serial killer that is cool and kills the bad guys, vampires living in small towns, murder and investigation programs, and backstabbing reality TV programs with a monetary payout for the winner. Remember that everything we allow into our brain, which is anything we are around, can and will infiltrate our daily thoughts and have the ability to contaminate our happy and positive nature.

Have you ever watched the news and afterwards, you felt sad and possibly a bit helpless in this world? Unfortunately, the news doesn't get high ratings by covering stories on how others are doing good things to better our planet. If the news covered all the positive things going on around us, the news would then be a wonderful source of community and education.

Some people believe that negativity on television doesn't affect them and that they are mentally strong enough to escape it. It's a good thought but not a true thought. We are all affected by what we see and hear. It doesn't matter how brilliant you are, we are all affected in one way or another. You might think that these types of stimuli do not affect you, if that is true, you are being affected more than others. The sheer denial of effect is scary and has no thought or reasoning based in reality. Denial is the stage of not admitting that something exists. If you need proof, next time you watch television, turn on the news and watch from the beginning and concentrate on your breathing and how you are feeling by watching this content.

Not only can television, films, and the radio cause negative thoughts within our minds and cause us more internal work to be done, so can reading some types of material. Recently, there were a few novels that I began to read that after a few chapters, I was determined to throw them away. These novels I speak of were both violent and negative. They didn't supply me with anything I need and I decided that I must get rid of them. Most books I read are enjoyable, entertaining, and sometimes very educational, but ever so often, a book gets back home and is none of the above, and instead of giving it away, I toss it in the recycle bin.

We are what we see and hear and because of that, we want to bestow onto ourselves things that will help us grow and thrive. When we fill our eyes and ears with positive stimuli, we are allowing ourselves to grow in a positive and productive manner. When we observe and monitor ourselves around certain stimuli, we are able to make conscious decisions and choices that better our lives and our subconscious minds.

It is important to fully appreciate the wonderful tool for success that each and every one of us has at our command and that tool is our mind. Theodore Roosevelt stated, "All the resources we need are in the mind." It is important to know that our conscious mind is only one-sixth of our brain's thinking and brainpower. The subconscious mind represents the other five-sixths of our thinking and brainpower.

The whole mind, both the conscious and the subconscious, possess the power and ability to solve any problem that may arise and can provide the ways and means to achieve our goals in life. The conscious mind holds between seven and ten pieces of information in its short-term memory. The subconscious mind stores all the knowledge you have ever acquired, which includes everything you have ever read, heard, thought or imagined. Brain researchers have estimated that your subconscious mind is so immense that it outweighs the conscious mind ten million to one.

The subconscious mind is the source of brilliance, great inspiration, and creativity. Because of that, we don't want to keep putting negative images and thoughts into our subconscious. We want to cultivate our subconscious mind and make it wiser and stronger. It is a scary thought, that our minds can be manipulated by television and radio. Everything we expose ourselves to can be placed in our subconscious and those subconscious thoughts can become subconscious beliefs. Thoughts become beliefs when you hear them enough and give those same thoughts energy, similar to the effect of affirmations but with a negative outcome. Those subconscious beliefs begin to affect our abilities to achieve our goals and desires. In order to try and achieve our goals, we may try affirmations but we still haven't penetrated into the subconscious mind to make necessary changes. In order to penetrate into the subconscious, we must work on changing our subconscious beliefs.

How to change our subconscious beliefs

1. Identify the negative beliefs or problem beliefs you are holding onto. In order to find the issues that exist inside of our subconscious minds, we must begin by writing down statements that we remember hearing from our parents while growing up. Write

down things that we say to ourselves and also write down things that we hear others tell us. Examples: I'm not pretty enough, money is evil, I'm not worthy, money doesn't grow on trees, I'm never going to be successful, I can't follow through with anything, etc. Once we put together this list, we can begin to test these beliefs to see how strong they are within us.

2. Testing these negative/problem beliefs. Looking at the list we have constructed, we can begin to test ourselves and see how deeply rooted these beliefs are within our subconscious mind. There are two ways I suggest testing to recognize how strong these beliefs are within your subconscious. The human body is a useful instrument that provides us with all types of information about ourselves.

Muscle testing or Applied Kinesiology is used to test muscles for weakness or strength and used as well on mental and or emotional issues and acknowledge how those issues are affecting the body. The body doesn't cover up as much as the mind. The body is more likely to give an honest assessment of what is going on instead of the thinking mind. The body will give truthful answers to issues that have been submerged in the subconscious. These physical answers will be unbiased and truthful and will help us examine these beliefs we have stored within the subconscious that need to be changed. Different muscles can be used for this test. The arms are the best and easiest to use but you do need a helper when doing it this way. Stretch one arm straight out in front of you or straight out to your side. Your partner in the process will tell you to resist as they press down on your arm and ask you questions. If your arm holds up to being pressed down, then the answer to the question is yes. If it doesn't hold up and gives in, then the answer is no. In order for the yes and no answers to work, we must ask direct questions. For example: Do you love yourself? Do you feel good about yourself?

The other way you can test yourself to see what is buried in your subconscious is by using a form of meditation. First, get yourself in a relaxed state of mind, focusing on your breathing and on your body, as discussed in chapter 4. You can then address each belief that you have written down and notice the way your body reacts to the statement. You can also recognize the internal dialogue that begins when you bring up each individual statement. Once you recognize each negative/ problem belief, you can release them, allow them to leave your body, and move past those non-working self-sabotaging beliefs. In order to effectively release these beliefs, you must replace the old with new positive beliefs.

3. Replacing negative beliefs with new positive beliefs. Once we are aware of our old beliefs and understand why we have these beliefs, we are able to reprogram our subconscious mind and replace those negative belief patterns with effective and strong positive beliefs. Sometimes the sudden understanding of why we react the way we do is enough to let go of these old beliefs and thought processes. When we are replacing these old beliefs, we must create a beautiful atmosphere for our mind. When we listen to music, we need to listen to music that raises us up and opens our minds. We all have certain music that makes us feel love, happiness, and tranquility; that is the music you need to be listening to. Better yet, if you can find music that has lyrics that go along the lines of what you want in your life, listen to that music.

When we listen to music with lyrics, we must choose the music that reflects the life and love we have for ourselves. When we listen to music that is negative or violent in nature, we are adding to our negative thought processes, and it is just more stuff that we have to deal with inside the subconscious mind.

We want to fill the subconscious with wonderful beautiful thoughts, not negative and undesirable thoughts and images. Music works very well to replace old beliefs because it is easiest to enter the mind. Music has the ability to slip into the mind, undetected. The vibrations and the tempo of the music allow it to flow into your mind quicker and easier than anything else. We've all had a song in our heads that we couldn't get rid of and we truly wanted to remove that song. Remember how easy it was to remember the beat, tempo, and lyrics of that song. That is why using music to help manifest new positive beliefs is so effective and quick. When you find a song that is positive and does speak of what you want in your life, you should listen to it over and over. It also helps to sing along with the song. When you sing the lyrics, the impact is even more powerful on your subconscious. You can even choose to write your own songs if you can't find what you are looking for.

Music can expand our minds and fulfill our hearts; by choosing wisely what we listen to, we can add to our quality of life. We don't allow our children to listen to explicit and violent lyrics because we don't think it is good for them; we should do the same and allow our minds to be shaped by beautiful lyrics.

Like music, TV can positively or negatively influence our lives. Since it is both auditory and visual, it can command our full focus and attention in an even greater way than music. When we choose programming that educates us on the environment, history, the arts, the world, etc., we are opening our mind to something that has merit and value. When we choose to watch something for its educational value, we are educating ourselves and strengthening our mind.

Sometimes, we may choose to watch something that makes us laugh or cry, but we must remember that all we view and hear is placed in the subconscious, so choose wisely.

4. Literature that you consume also gets stored in the subconscious mind. What we choose to read should be worthy of our time. When something is worthy, it has fundamental value and supplies you with something in return. We should use our time wisely by choosing uplifting, educational, and helpful literature that awakens our minds and senses, to create the life we need and desire. When we read things that broaden our minds, we are educating ourselves and creating a wealth of knowledge. When we read something

that uplifts us and makes us feel good, we are enhancing that feeling of being content and in turn being positive about our life and our surroundings, and we strengthen ourselves physically, mentally, emotionally, and spiritually. We are spending our time enhancing our lives to understand ourselves, the reasons for doing things, and how to create what we want in our lives.

Of course, we also can read for entertainment, but we must define it as such and realize that some of this entertainment may cause negative thoughts within the subconscious. There are countless books on the market about the end of the world coming in 2012. Whether or not these books are based on any factual evidence is irrelevant. What is relevant is the impact these books have on the people that read them and take this information to heart. I have a friend that is reading one such book and he talks about it every morning over coffee. What a way to start your day! I can pinpoint the time he began reading the book because of the changes to his demeanor and personality. He has become more negative and disinterested in life. There is nothing more negative than contemplating the end of the world every morning before work and reading about it every night before you go to bed. The fear factor is overwhelming and that is what sells these types of books. Fear is something used to keep people down and scared of everyone and everything around them. This feeling of fear can dominate our lives and fill us with hatred and ignorance.

Fear is a negative-based feeling that resonates at a very low frequency. This frequency creates no happiness and no positive returns. People begin to think that if the end of the world is really upon us, it does not matter what we do, because nothing matters anyway - a very sad thought.

We have an endless array of choices to pick from with regards to our actions and our futures. By changing our daily viewing habits and switching to positive content, we will begin to change our thought patterns and our internal feelings. If we consciously observe our feelings and thoughts and work to remove negative thoughts from our minds, we will create a more positive environment for others and ourselves. By working on ourselves and filling our minds with positive stimuli, we will create a happy and peaceful state of mind. When you create that for yourself, others will follow your example and do the same. Before we know it, we have a society of positive conscious people. When we are conscious and aware, we can move past any obstacle and positively fulfill our chosen destiny. Instead of 2012 being viewed as the deadline for the end of the world, I believe it to be a goal for a much-needed shift in consciousness, which we all can help cultivate and bring about, and benefit from. We can all be co-creators that allow this world to move in a positive and loving direction that works together and runs smoothly. Why not? We are all in control of our decisions and our actions. No one else can make you happy; no one else can open your eyes to conscious living except you. Your life is in your hands. We all have choices in life and these choices can help us, hurt us, or keep us stagnated. You can show by example to others and create a lasting impression within their minds, but in the end, everyone has to make their own choice.

A t-shirt I saw recently had the words: Shift Happens, on the front. Many people believe that there will be a polar shift in 2012 that will bring about the end of time. Instead of a polar shift, what about a shift in consciousness? If we shift our lives and begin to live true to ourselves, we can cause a huge shift in consciousness and create the world we have always wanted. We have the ability to change the world; we just have to do it! By making the necessary changes to our daily life, we will make an impact on all around us and that will cause a surge within the community and the world. Because we are all linked together, the ability for the social consciousness to shift to a positive state, and produce a significant impact, is within our grasp. By taking the first step, we can begin to see a huge change in the people and the world around us. Also, we will have been helpful in the world's conscious shift. The world will awaken from its subconscious driven coma and come to life as an enlightened, positive, expansive, and conscious human race.

How many times do you turn on the television and see shows reporting about yet another celebrity who has made bad choices? We have grown into such an unconscious society that we aren't even interested in the real news; we are interested in gossip. Why have we allowed our news programs to fill our brains with stuff we don't need and don't want? The reason the networks report this is for higher ratings because, yes, this is what we want to hear about. We are so busy wondering about celebrities and their sordid lives that we don't pay attention to the things happening around us. We must wake up and stop living our lives through others. When we choose to live our lives through others, we stop living our own life.

You are the only person that can make your life grand and interesting; watching others do it will not help. It only takes away from the time we have to make our life something special and meaningful. We all have the ability to have the life we have always dreamed of, but it takes effort on our part to make that dream a reality.

We all deserve our relaxation time and that time should be used to better ourselves and make ourselves stronger and happier people. Whether we are watching television, reading a book, or listening to music, we need to select our viewing and listening choices wisely so we create and live that true life we want and need. Better yet, remember that you can choose to work out, take a walk, jog, play tennis, write, learn to play an instrument, play with your children and your pets.

Personal Reflection and Blog:

What television shows do you watch? Do you feel at peace after viewing these shows? If not, why do you choose to watch them?

Do you use a DVR to record your favorite shows? Does using the DVR help you to limit your television time?

Are their any particular television or radio programs that you feel expand your mind and help to make your life better?

What are some hobbies that you have taken up in the replacement of television?

What do you listen to on your way to work?

What do you listen to when working out, jogging or running?
Is there a particular piece of music that raises your spirits when you are sad or depressed?

Is there a particular piece of music that gives you true joy to listen to? What is that music? Do you listen to it often?

Chapter 9:

DOING WHAT IS RIGHT FOR YOU... WITHIN MODERATION

What's right for you? What we truly want and need is difficult to fully determine and understand. Something that is right for us should be congruent to achieving and living our true lives. When we are working to better our lives we can use goal setting as an excellent way to inspire us, and track our progress.

Often, we set goals that can't be realistically achieved. An unrealistic goal is one that you can't visualize yourself achieving, you really don't expect it to happen, and it doesn't immediately move you into positive action. A realistic goal is one based in reason and grounded in personal confidence, strength, determination, and definite willpower. In order to successfully achieve our goals, we must have an emotional and compelling reason for achieving them. Our goals must move us into immediate action. When we create unrealistic goals, we are making wishes that have no commitment for fulfillment.

Commitment requires belief in our goal and belief in one's self, which will be pursued with definite direction, focus, and steady perseverance.

Many times we try and set goals in our lives to eliminate an activity or thing but instead of elimination, we find ourselves deeper in it then before. This occurs because we didn't set realistic goals; instead we set an unattainable goal that we could not stick to. Instead of complete elimination of alcohol from our diet, which in many cases is an unrealistic goal, and in certain situations unnecessary, we should examine the concept of moderation. Moderation is the process of eliminating or lessening extremes. Essentially, moderation is a life principle. Going back to ancient Greek times, the temple of Apollo at Delphi bore the inscription: Meden Agan, which means, Nothing in excess. To do something in moderation means to not do it to excess.

If we practice moderation on a daily basis, we can allow ourselves many options that we didn't have before. When we live within moderation, we allow ourselves a variety of experiences, perhaps some not completely beneficial, but we back it up with the majority of things that are good for us. When we examine drinking, eating, etc., We must evaluate how much we can safely do without causing hazard to others and self.

In order for the concept of moderation to work in your life, you first must be able to verbalize what in your life is most important, and name your responsibilities. Family, children, pets, friends, job, hobbies, taking care of yourself, etc, are the most important elements in your life and are also your responsibilities. These things that we consider important in our lives must be fulfilled for our lives to be successful. At this time, take out that notebook we were using in previous chapters and start a new page. On the top of the page, write the title: Life Responsibilities, and begin writing down your personal responsibilities in order of importance. These responsibilities must be your priority, and you must plan to accomplish them with daily dedication. When we place an order of operations on our daily lives and create a schedule of responsibilities, we are then able to use moderation with regards to the unnecessary things that we allow in our lives. Those unnecessary things could be drinking alcohol, smoking a cigarette, talking on the phone, playing video games, spending time on Facebook, doing drugs both illegal and prescription, watching television, gambling/betting, etc. The above activities have become a problem when we allow them to take over our lives. If we are taking care of our business and living true to ourselves, we will be doing what we need to do to make our lives successful. After correctly fulfilling our responsibilities on a daily basis, we are then allowed what I refer to as personal time within moderation. Basically after all responsibilities have been fulfilled, you have time to do what you want to do with your time, within moderation. Realizing that you have responsibilities tomorrow, you must have fun within responsible moderate limits. With regards to everything you do, if done to excess, you cause an unbalance that eventually causes pain in your life. In order to have personal clarity and to be empowered, you must do what is right for you. For some, doing what is right for you means NOT doing certain things: drinking all night, playing video games for ten hours straight, gambling, etc. Unwinding and relaxing is healthy and keeps us balanced but with regards to these activities, you can quickly spiral out of control.

If your life becomes unbalanced in one area, it creates problems in all other areas of your life. If you are a workaholic, you will make less time for other important life responsibilities and activities, and you will cause yourself to be dissatisfied with life. This unbalance will generate other problems in your life, and will eventually take you away from finding yourself and your true and whole happiness. When we practice moderation, we allow balance in our lives.

Through the use of moderation, we are able to slow down or even stop something we are doing that isn't bettering us. It becomes something that we don't want to do anymore or as much, because we have found our true life, our true calling, not because we can't do that thing anymore, but instead we have chosen not to. When we have realized our true calling and our true self, we no longer want to fill our time with the things that don't better us and don't bring us closer to our true self. When you spend time and energy fulfilling your obligations, responsibilities, and moving yourself closer to achieving your life goals, you are no longer constantly thinking of doing that thing that moves you farther away from your true self. Over time, as you get closer to achieving your life goals, and experience the excitement and energy that this gives you, you will eliminate the need and cravings you have that make you want to engage in behavior that moves you in the opposite direction. The closer we get to achieving our goals, the less we want to get off target.

Just because you choose to not do something anymore doesn't change the fact that you think you want to do it. When you truly look within yourself and figure out why you do that certain something, you can then moderate or stop that beause of the knowledge you derive from yourself and not from fear or disillusionment. By going inside ourselves to seek the answers for why we do something, we are able to examine our motives and emotions and establish a healthy moderation, or stop this activity in its entirety; taking this approach will result in self-control through self-knowledge, as opposed to fear.

In order to get to the root of why we do something, we must take an honest look at ourselves and the particular chosen activity or thing.

We must ask ourselves deep personal questions and allow ourselves to come forth with truthful and honest answers, no matter how they sound or make us feel.

1. What am I getting out of this particular activity?

When we truly delve into why we do something, we must examine and understand what we are getting from this experience. Is this activity allowing for physical, mental, or spiritual growth? Is this activity aiding in the unwinding and relaxation process in my life? Does this activity charge my batteries and allow me to take care of my responsibilities? Or does this activity take away from me and leave me tired? Do I spend too much energy dealing with this activity in my life? Is this activity becoming a chore or another responsibility?

2. Why do I choose this for myself?

Why have I selected this activity for myself?
Why have I allowed this to occupy my time?
Am I truly doing what is best for me?
Does this help me in some way?
Does this activity add balance to my life?
If we aren't doing what is best for us, do we realize and see that?

3. How true am I?

When you drink, gamble, or other, how true am I being to myself? Is this who I am? By the way, who am I?

What do I want for my life?

Is there more to me than this?

If this activity is beginning to take over your life, you must learn/remember who you are and begin to separate from this activity.

Can you remember a time that you weren't involved with this particular activity?

How is this adding to you as a person?

4A. Who are the others involved?

If there are people around me when I'm involved in this activity, are they truly there for me, do they have what's best for me in their minds and hearts and are they acting that way? For the most part, we participate in most activities with others, so look around and seriously ask yourself questions about your friends. Sometimes when we get involved in an activity, our friends are there to agree with us. But we must ask ourselves honestly, if these people we have chosen to spend time with and do this activity with, are truly our friends, with our personal welfare in mind.

The people we choose to have around us can benefit us greatly by truly caring about us and wanting what's best for us. Also, true friends will help us see the truth and not allow us to lie to ourselves and others. Many times when we are doing something antithetical to our wellbeing, our friends will step in and talk to us. True friends will not allow us to believe in our lies.

On the other hand, if the people we choose to spend time with do not have our best interests at heart, they may enable us to believe our own lies. When we believe lies of others and/or our own, we do what is wrong for us. Instead of looking at our life truthfully, we begin to see a skewed image that validates the lies we are telling ourself and the lies that others are telling us.

4B. On the flip side, am I doing this activity solo?

If you are participating in an activity solo, you must ask yourself if this is healthy. For example, if you are drinking by yourself, this particular act of drinking has become an antisocial event. Many times, if you have to do something alone or feel you have to hide doing it, that thing you are doing is most likely unhealthy and not adding to you as a person. Why do you feel you have to partake in this activity by yourself? Are you hiding from thers? Are you hiding from yourself? Are you hiding this because you believe others will not accept you doing this or behaving this way?

5. Can I stop this activity at any time?

When we take a serious look at something we do and really examine why we do it, we must step back with honesty and determine if we can truly moderate this activity by ourselves or do we need professional guidance. How many times in a day do you think about this activity? Is it dominating your thoughts in a way that is preventing you from accomplishing your priorities?

In order to stop the constant thought of this activity, you must fill your mind and day with the activities at hand. You must get centered in the moment and tackle what you have to do now. If you stay centered in the moment, the constant thought of the other activity will dissipate, and you will have more power over it and more balance in your life.

Otherwise, if you are going through your day constantly thinking about doing that activity, you have not clearly examined your motivation for

LIVE YOUR TRUE LIFE

doing it. You may be choosing this activity because you are trying to forget something, or deal with sadness or abandonment; you need to go within to find that out. Once you have figured out the reason for your need for escape, you are able to ask yourself serious questions.

First, does this activity help you escape or to avoid dealing with your feelings? Are you choosing to run from your feelings or cover them up? If so, why? Does this activity get you closer to your true feelings or does it push you farther away? If it allows you to get closer to your feelings, how does it do that? If this activity moves you farther away from dealing with your feelings, why have you chosen this route? These feelings must be dealt with now before they manifest into something larger and harder to come to grips with. If you are struggling with issues, you might want to seek the help of a professional counselor or psychologist, who can help you understand or illuminate your feelings, motivations, and personal needs.

When we allow something to take over our lives, we have basically allowed that thing to take our identity. It's a type of identity theft because we are no longer that person with all those amazing facets, we are a one-sided person that has to have that certain thing to live and breathe. Eventually we are only living to do that thing and if we are not doing it, we are thinking about it. The vicious cycles begins when you wake up and do that thing, get nothing done with regards to the rest of your life, and then sit around and wait to do that thing again, paying no attention to anything else in your life. You may even be taking care of your responsibilities, but upon truthful examination they may be enabling you to return to the activity, or they may even be the cause of your desire to return to that activity. For example, a drug user maybe going to work every day, but it is only to allow him to afford his habit; and he may be driven to this habit out of discontent with his current employment.

When we allow things to get out of balance, and waste all our energy and thoughts on that particular activity or thing, we have dismissed our true self and have turned our back on our true life. In order to have balance in our lives, we must exercise our innate ability to self-regulate. Self-regulation is most important when working to maintain a healthy lifestyle of moderation. When we self-regulate, we are constantly striving towards goals we have set for ourselves. When we get off task or are unsuccessful we need to redirect our energies back towards our life goals. When we self-regulate, we take on an active role, not a passive role, in order to make our lives better and attain the life goals we have set out for ourselves. The goals we set for ourselves motivate us and focus our attention toward something we want to achieve. When we are truly motivated towards a goal, our anticipated fulfillment of that goal provides the needed motivation to continue on until the goal is reached. When we are setting goals for our self, we must be specific. Our goals need to be accurately defined. Our goals must be challenging but not overwhelming. We've all made goals for ourselves that were so unrealistic that there was no way we could successfully achieve them. The goals we set forth for ourselves should be difficult but not impossible. We will put forth effort and focus our attention and resources in order to achieve our difficult but realistic goal. We will not set goals that are overwhelming and out of our sphere of attainment because we will only fail and be discouraged with ourselves.

When we define our goals, we must put a time frame on them. Are your goals long term or short term in nature? When we are dealing with long-term goals, we should divide them into smaller goals or milestones in order to stay motivated and positively focused.

In order to successfully attain our life goals, we must use positive reinforcement; so once you have reached a milestone, or completed your goal, you should allow yourself some time for a treat. With the use of positive reinforcement, we are able to put the concept of moderation into practice in our daily lives.

Many times we can change our lives on our own, but when we are wrestling with tougher issues and addictions, the help from a support group can add another level of support and motivation. A support group could be on-line or attending local meetings on a weekly basis. Realizing that you are not alone is a wonderful space to be in when dealing with addiction and the desire to change and manifest a different more complete life.

Many times we never look deeply into why we are addicted to something, we are just down in it. We never fully look into ourselves to realize why we are attached to this activity or thing. Addiction to a substance is difficult, but what are you getting out of doing that substance and is it still giving you what you want or thought you wanted? When you finally take a straight look at something and see it for what it is, and who you truly are, and why you choose to do it, you are able to unravel the mystery and take away the interest and see it for what it truly is. We as humans can become addicted to just about anything, including drugs, alcohol, work, love, people, food, etc. We become addicted to these things because we feel as if they are filling a void we have within. Unfortunately, these addictions cannot fill anything. They are being used as a masking tool to prevent you from exploring the void and understanding why it exists and what it is made up of. The only thing that can fill an emotional void is truth and honesty not a bandage or self-medication that is but another masking tool that we have fabricated to cover up our emotions and hurt self. Once we realize that these voids will not just go away or be covered up, we are able to go honestly into them and understand the reason for their existence and the reason for our previous self denial.

There are things within all of us that we don't want to look at. But once we begin examining these things and understanding them, we are able to understand our motivations and ourselves more clearly without self-denial.

Personal Reflection and Blog:

Are their things in your life that you need
to moderate?

What are they?

Have they disrupted the rest of your life?

Have they caused you to not fulfill your
responsibilities?

Do you feel that your life is balanced?

Do you have any voids in your life? Do you feel
that you are trying to mask a void with something or
someone else?

Do you feel that something in your life has gotten
out of hand and has formed into an addiction?

What is that addiction?

When did it begin?

Can you stop this addiction?

Have you tried stopping this addiction before?

What do you need, to move past this addiction and
get back to yourself?

Do you feel emotionally organized?

What are your daily responsibilities? Outside
of your daily responsibilities, what other
responsibilities do you have?

Personal Reflection and Blog: (continued)

With regards to goals, what goals do you have for yourself?

Have you chosen to not set goals for yourself?

If you do have personal goals, are they long term in nature? If they are, do you have milestones within the goal to keep you motivated? Do you feel that you are working daily to achieve your goals?

On completion of a milestone or goal, do you allow yourself a treat? If so, what is that treat?

FINAL WORD:

Live Your True Life is an instruction book written to take the guesswork out of life and to move or eliminate the obstacles we have in our daily lives. After reading this book and putting the theories into practice, all of a sudden life becomes easier, more manageable, and ultimately more fulfilling.

When writing this book, I wanted it to be a handbook for life that is easy to follow, understand, and put into practice. I hope you enjoy reading this book as much as I enjoyed writing it.

If you have any comments or questions, feel free to email me at liveyourtruelife@me.com. This book is not just a book; it is grounded within a community: liveyourtruelife.com is a wonderful tool that enables you to go a step further and meet other likeminded people. It also allows you to share your life and experiences with others. Thank you again for becoming an active participant in the Live Your True Life family and more importantly in your own life.